Now, I AM

KIM BARDER

Edited by Lexi Mohney
Cover Design by Simona Manenti

An Imprint for GracePoint Publishing (www.GracePointPublishing.com)

GracePoint Matrix, LLC
624 S. Cascade Ave, Suite 201
Colorado Springs, CO 80903
www.GracePointMatrix.com
Email: Admin@GracePointMatrix.com
SAN # 991-6032

Library of Congress Control Number: 2023939455

ISBN: (Paperback) 978-1-955272-93-3
eISBN: 978-1-955272-94-0

Books may be purchased for educational, business, or sales promotional use.
For bulk order requests and price schedule contact:
Orders@GracePointPublishing.com

Dedication

I would like to express my love, deepest gratitude, and appreciation to my father. Thank you for an amazing life together. Although you are no longer with me in the physical, you live and dwell in my heart now and always. I take great comfort in this knowing. And yes, you are still the smartest, most handsome guy ever. I'll love you forever.

Love's eternal promise,
Ever so true.
That which you love,
Can never leave you.

For it dwells in the sacredness,
Of your open, pure heart,
Whispering softly to you now,
"We can never be apart."

Just a blip in time,
That felt to you like forever,
In the eternal dance we dance,
We are destined to be together.

Together once again,
Of that you can be sure,
Laughing, playing, and loving,
In a time we knew before.

No, there is never an end,
And therein lies the beauty of it all,
And when this becomes your truth,
Never a tear again shall fall.

I love you forever.

It's all about what lights you up,
And your favorite song.
It's all about smiling, laughing out loud,
And dancing all night long.

It's all about being with those,
Who love you 24/7, 365,
It's all about doing always,
What makes you feel alive.

It's all about kindness and compassion,
Yes, it's about that, too,
Always serving others,
As if they were you.

It's all about knowing who you are,
Who you've always been.
It's all about knowing the light,
Has already secured the win.

It's all about speaking your truth,
And standing firm in your power.
It's all about rallying for Mother Earth,
In her most needed hour.

It's all about you,
For you are the one.
It's all about you healing all within,
So all can only see the sun.

Table of Contents

Letter to the Reader

This is my story.

Welcome, and thank you for being here. What you are about to read is the story of my awakening. It is the beginning journey of my conscious awareness into my own ascension.

As my story unfolds you may recognize parts of yourself or experiences within this story that may be similar to your experiences.

You have brought this book into your awareness now, at this very moment. It is my wish that as you read the pages that follow, you discover why it is you have done so.

As you read this book, I hope that you allow yourself to open to infinite, divine possibilities of what you believe can be. What follows in these pages occurred. It is truth; it is my truth that I now share with you.

When one awakens and has transcendental experiences with divine beings of love and light, it can at first challenge all belief systems. These experiences can then allow for an opening to occur—a spaciousness that allows for the possibility of a new way of being, a new reality. In fact, this is exactly why it occurs. It is an opportunity for you to begin to peel off layers of conditioning that will enable you to ultimately reveal a pearl. This pearl is the true essence of who it is that you are, deep within.

This book was a co-creation, as is everything in the universe. I surrendered the writing of this book to my own "I AM Presence" and the words then flowed through me onto these pages. The Divine often uses repetition to drive certain points home for the reader, so they may grasp fully any important concepts. There are experiences within these pages, which include beautiful beings of light such as angels, Ascended Masters, and spirit guides.

You will also find divinely inspired poetry throughout this book. These poems were gifts from The Divine given to me to share with others at different stages along my journey, as well as within this book. For me, poetry is yet another channel The Divine works through to express its messages of love and light.

All things are truly possible, and as you allow yourself to open up to those infinite, divine possibilities, miracles can, and will, occur.

Shall we begin?

Introduction

My Aunt Sallie passed away from a surgery complication. If anyone wore the pants in our family, it was her. She could command an army if she needed something done, and she never hesitated in grabbing the nearest person and roping them into accomplishing whatever tasks she had on her plate for that day.

Though many of her authoritative (but always loving) characteristics were endearing, she meant the most to me because of the love and support she offered when I lost my mother and sister earlier in life.

So, when it came to her funeral, I was more than just a bit upset. All I wanted, after the exhaustion of burying her, was to rest.

My husband was already in bed, having fallen asleep quickly, and when I climbed in beside him, the sheets welcomed me.

I was dozing off, allowing my mind to drift away from the emotions of the day, when I felt a punch to my right arm. My husband was lying right next to me, and besides the steady sound of breathing, he hadn't moved.

I froze in fear. Was someone in the room I hadn't noticed in my daze?

I roused my husband. "What was that? Did you feel it?" I asked.

My husband, half asleep, responded, "What are you talking about, Kim? It's late."

"I'm serious. Someone punched me in the arm; didn't you feel it?"

He took a deep breath and let it out slowly, clearly mustering patience with me after a long day. "No. Now, can we go to sleep, please?"

A small frown creased my brow as he turned over and fell asleep again.

I, on the other hand, could not fall asleep. Something or someone definitely hit me square in the arm. It was as real as the light snores coming from my husband.

I got out of bed and looked all around the room, flicking on the bathroom light so I could see a bit better while trying not to wake my husband again. When it was clear there was no one else in the room, and there were no fallen objects on the floor, I woke my husband up again.

"I swear, something definitely hit me, and it's really starting to freak me out," I told him.

He sighed. "All right, is there anything I can do?"

I blinked at him. I wasn't sure. I didn't know what *could* be done about it, but I was beginning to become unglued.

"I'm leaving the bathroom light on, then," I said.

He nodded before rolling over to sleep soundly through the rest of the night.

I lay back down, but it was hard for me to settle. Whatever struck me *hurt* and it scared me. I didn't want to be hit again by the mysterious presence.

As I calmed down enough to begin drifting into sleep, a peaceful knowing came over me. My intuition told me Aunt Sallie punched me in the arm to let me know she was all right.

In my grogginess, I wondered, *Can that be?* We had just attended my aunt's funeral. If her presence was here, it was more than my mind could possibly comprehend. *But that would be like her, to give a quick punch,* I thought. That would have most definitely been a way she would have expressed her care and love.

Though it caught my attention, I could hardly fathom the possibility, especially since I'd had plenty of other relatives pass before Aunt Sallie and none of them had attempted communication after their deaths. Aunt Sallie was the first—*if* that was what it was.

No, wherever Aunt Sallie was, I doubted I was at the top of her list of people to haunt from beyond the grave—if that were even a thing. And I was able to ignore it long enough to drift off to sleep for a little while longer.

Changes ever present,
Swirling through time I go.
Sifting and sorting,
Leaving some behind as I grow.

The old self dissolves completely,
To birth the new.
I turn around,
And where are you?

Ever evolving and expanding,
To higher light.
My soul greets me and tells me,
"You got this, it's all right."

There's no going back now,
Nor would I if I could.
I don't live in the world anymore,
Of "do this because you should."

There are new, glorious moments now,
And still more to unfold,
Treasure them I do,
As if they were gold.

Surreal is an understatement.
Where is the one I used to be?
Blown away in the wind, she is,
For the magnificent chance to be.

I AM grateful.

Chapter One

The "I AM Presence"

*I*magine you are standing in the middle of a candy store as a young child. However, there is a catch: There is a paper bag placed over your head and you do not know you are standing in the middle of a candy store where the most delicious candies you could ever try and experience are right there, all around you.

When you occupy your physical body in this life, the paper bag is akin to the veil of incarnation. This "veil" causes you to forget you are the creator of your reality. You forget how powerful you are and that you can create and have all you desire. Your own divinity is temporarily hidden from you by this veil.

We, the human collective, did this on purpose during incarnation to have a particular Earth experience. However, the time has arrived to take the metaphorical paper bag off and remember your own divinity and all the blessings that come with that level of awareness and elevated consciousness. We do not know we are missing pieces of our experience until the veil is lifted. Then the truth of our multidimensional sensory deprivation is exposed, and the knowing-ness of our divinity, our essence, is able to shine through.

By removing the paper bag a world of everything we could ever desire or envision for ourselves is revealed. The beauty of the metaphorical paper bag is that we are the ones holding it in place. Therefore, by allowing ourselves to open to infinite possibilities, we are able to see the magnificence waiting for us in every aspect of our lives.

So, what are we waiting for?

It is important to note that each of us awakens in the perfect divine time and order that serves our highest good. There is a whole, grand, divine design that we are each a part of, and our own personal awakening journey is part of that tapestry. Removing the paper bag and beginning our awakening journeys can feel a bit unnerving because it is unknown and new to us. However, there truly is nothing to fear, and The Divine, our own "I AM Presence" is always in command of the process, as well as the timing of when that process begins.

Fear is *false evidence appearing real.* We may fear our awakening because we are familiar with the world we have known, the world inside our metaphorical bags. Many refer to this space as the comfort zone, but few are ever truly comfortable there. After all, one may grow up in an environment of lack and deprivation, which is an example of life under the bag, but is that better than taking it off and stepping into an awareness of divine perfection and knowing?

By changing the name *comfort zone* to *zone of familiarity*, it becomes clear that the space we remain in, the bag we keep in place that masks the truth of our existence, is only there because it is familiar. We often stay trapped in an uncomfortable world because we know how to handle and navigate it. The Divine is constantly sending messages and offering opportunities for us to expand our consciousness, allowing us to see from that highest divine perspective. Until you awaken to universal truth, you will keep having experiences and will be given ample opportunities to open to your true, divine, loving self.

When you reach this highest state of consciousness, this knowing that all of creation and all of existence is the "I AM Presence," that you are one with, then no human creation has the power to control or disturb you; therefore, fear of the unfamiliar becomes insignificant. Knowing the entire universe is love is the first step to conquering any fear. The only reason any disturbance makes an appearance in our lives is to give us an opportunity, in that moment, to recognize it as the "I AM Presence," the only solver of any perceived problem that you could ever possibly encounter, and to then surrender to it.

Our divine, mighty, all-knowing self is referred to as the "I AM Presence," the individualized divine aspect of each of us. It has many names including "I AM Presence," soul, Source, core essence, higher self, and more. It is the connection to the Source of creation and the space of manifestation and desire, but more than that, it is the ever-present and eternal source of our being, love, and life.

Merging and aligning with your "I AM Presence" is important because it is your source for everything. When you identify your connection to the Divine Source, you can then see how you connect to All That Is in your universe. The truth uncovered through the "I AM Presence" reveals that there is only God—the "I AM Presence"—in action, everywhere, present now.

Our Source connection, the "I AM Presence," is the individualized, divine aspect of us. When we fully merge and bond with it and become the full embodiment of it, we gain access to all the divine, infinite knowledge and wisdom in all of creation.

"Come take a walk with me."
I hear it say.
"There is absolutely nothing,
To be done today.

Just be silent,
And hold my hand,
And I will whisk you away,
To a far-off land.

We'll be there in an instant,
Just as quick as you choose it to be.
Come now, my beloved,
And take this journey with me.

No bags are needed to be packed,
And no other will come along.
For this is a love story,
And only you and I compose this song.

An eternal embrace,
We now begin,
Deep within the heart,
We journey together, within."

This is a good thing to recognize and be aware of because it highlights the vast potential of any one individual through bonding with and attuning to the "Mighty I AM Presence." If we align with our "I AM Presence" and thus the collective divinity of everything, we have a chance to open ourselves up to a grander understanding of our own infinite possibilities.

As we embody our "I AM Presence" we have the opportunity, through it, to live out our individual soul missions for this lifetime with pure, divine clarity, and on purpose.

Regaining our connection to and understanding that we are one with our "I AM Presence" is paramount to manifesting and co-creating our dreams and desires in this life. However, taking the proverbial paper bag off our heads may at first seem like a daunting task. After all, having done things a certain way for so very long, there are plenty of unknowns to changing our perception and ways of existing and interacting with ourselves and with those around us.

As you awaken, remember to be gentle with yourself and do your best to make everything you are being and doing an act of self-love. As you care for yourself you are also caring for others, Mother Earth, and all of creation itself, this is because we are all one.

There are many different and helpful ways of stilling the mind to give greater access to your "I AM Presence." Grounding, meditation, yoga, affirmations, and prayer can bring a sense of calm and open us up to the potential for more. But above all, focusing always on love will always serve your highest good and the highest good of all, simultaneously.

Accessing your own "I AM Presence" through self-love is the key to living a more healthy, peaceful, joyful, abundant, and harmonious life.

Separation consciousness is turning to the external world to seek answers, instead of turning inward to the infinite divine wisdom that already dwells in you. It is a forgetting of your own "I AM

Presence" and a belief that you are somehow separate from your Source. It is a belief that you are somehow separate from all things.

When we access our "I AM Presence," we are finally able to get comfortable with our true selves. Our disconnection from others is directly linked to our disconnection from our own "I AM Presence." By identifying limiting beliefs, toxic patterns, and old ways of being, we are better able to identify the areas of our lives that require our love, acceptance, time, and attention so we can nurture ourselves and heal.

Embracing, loving, and being in full acceptance of all your emotions, as they arise in your experience, allows them to move through your energy field with ease and grace. All suffering is caused by resisting that which is showing up in your life. It shows up to give you the opportunity to love and accept it as the divine perfection it always is.

Once you love and accept those parts of yourself you have denied in the past, they can quickly move on. They no longer have to come to you and manifest in your experience. The only reason they come into your experience is to give you the gift and opportunity to love them as part of the All, the "I AM Presence" they are. Many of our outdated beliefs and ways of thinking are products of bygone eras. They belong to societies that adopted them for means of production, profit, and survival, and we simply do not live in that type of world anymore.

Another way to start removing the paper bag is to open yourself up to curiosity. When you allow yourself to see things in a new light, with innocent perception, a whole new perspective can blossom. Problems you once thought impossible reveal solutions you could have never imagined. Seeing the world with childlike wonder leads to experiencing the miraculous.

Something powerful that is not often taught to newly awakened beings is the strength in asking for help from The Divine and intending and affirming that which you desire as if you already have it, because you do. You are already one with all things as the beloved "I AM Presence" you are. Asking is overlooked because many people have been conditioned throughout their lives to believe they'll never get what they want even if they make a direct pass for it. This conditioning often starts at a very young age and is taught to us by typically trusted sources like our parents or other adult figures in our lives. There is no blame here; our parents and loved ones did the best they could with the level of consciousness that they were at the time.

Amazingly, the thread of *not* asking runs so deep, the origin of this belief is lost to time itself. But the belief is reinforced because the outer world is a reflection of what is happening inside of us. If you are peaceful on the inside, your experience of your own life will be peaceful as well. Whatever is going on inside of you, in terms of your beliefs about things, is always mirrored back to you.

This is where the "I AM Presence" comes into play. If you can learn to open and turn to this higher aspect of yourself for everything, you'll gain better trust and resilience to that which doesn't seem to be going your way. Not only that, but as you merge more and more with your "I AM Presence" and gain more clarity, you'll be better able to intend and manifest your desires.

The "I AM Presence" is one of infinite wisdom and unconditional love. It is who you are and is always ready to direct you toward your greatest desires. The comfort and connection you feel with yourself as you merge with "I AM Presence" is that feeling which brings forth your wildest dreams and your deepest desires. Your "I AM Presence" is the breath in your lungs, and it's the beating of your heart. It is your one true source of everything and all.

Because it is the divine, individualized aspect of Source itself, how the "I AM Presence" looks is different for everyone. Think of the "I AM Presence" as the angelic-looking version of you. This beautiful being of infinite love and light is constantly waiting for you to ask for its guidance and assistance. The sooner you turn to it and surrender to its divine wisdom, giving it your full obedience and authority, the sooner you will begin to manifest your desires. Your "I AM Presence" is your source for abundance, joy, bliss, happiness, wealth, peace, freedom, harmony, balance, and success along with so much more. It is, in essence, the end of all your suffering, if you allow it to be.

The reason you can end all your heartache and suffering by turning to your "I AM Presence" is because all suffering is caused by disconnection from your Source. Love is your supply for everything and all. When you believe you are somehow separate from your source, from the love you are, your experience will reflect that. You are the creator of your own reality, and as such, your every command is always answered with an emphatic *yes*. An ease will begin to arise as you navigate any difficult situation through your own "I AM Presence." This occurs because you have placed all your trust and faith in your own "I AM Presence," who is always serving your highest good. The Earthly experience is meant to be one of co-creation—between you and your "I AM Presence."

There are a couple of ways to communicate full surrender to the "I AM Presence" in order to gain the benefit of the connection. First is to give over your complete authority to it. By relinquishing, you are giving your "I AM Presence" command of any situation. However it works out, it is in the hands of The Divine, and you can lean into knowing your "I AM Presence" will take care of you and any situation with absolute divine perfection, always for your highest good and the highest good of all.

Second, you can better connect to your "I AM Presence" by giving your full obedience to it. Now, I know obedience is a tricky subject because no one wants to be subservient. When I speak about obedience, what I mean is to follow the divine guidance that is being given to you directly from your own "I AM Presence," which is always for your highest good. We can sometimes make it difficult on ourselves by ignoring the path of least resistance we've been directed to by our higher knowing, which loves us unconditionally beyond measure. We could have already made it to the proverbial finish line and manifested our desires had we followed along with our divine guidance.

You can also choose to use the powerful word *Victory* in your affirmations. When you desire to manifest something, your acknowledgment of the *Victory* of it is the completion of all the energy you require to produce the manifestation. It is a pressure that compels your manifestation to be finished. It is an energy of completion.

For example, you can apply this to your "supply"—all that you desire and require for your joyful life. You can keep affirming and intending and "charging" your business, your home, your activities, all your affairs, and all you choose, with the *Victory* of your boundless supply released into physical use.

When you are charging something, you are bringing forth a particular energy into something. Since the entire universe is love energy, a vibration, a frequency, when you charge it with the energy of *Victory,* you are then charging it with that specific quality, which is the energy of completion by its definition. When you do this, your "I AM Presence" turns on the pressure, seeing it to its completion, which is bringing it forth into your physical use. Anytime you desire something to be manifested for your physical use, you demand the *Victory* of that supply released for that definite thing.

The Ascended Masters, who are divine, enlightened beings and who have had the experience of being in a physical body on Earth, have said you must say the word *Victory* and give conscious knowledge and use of the word *Victory* if, in fact, you want *Victory.* In another example, if you want the Ascended Masters' protection, then demand and intend everything in your being and world be ever charged with the invincible *Victory* of the Ascended Masters—of the Ascended Masters' invincible protection of everything in your being and world.

The Great Ascended Masters of Light have also explained the safeguard of using the word 'victory' in the intentions you set forth. For example, when you call for the Ascended Masters' *Victory* of your boundless supply to be released, it not only brings the more instantaneous action of the energy of your outer self to perfect it and release the supply, but if you call for the Ascended Masters' *Victory*, it also carries protection. The Ascended Masters want to assure us no matter what we choose and desire to manifest in this world, we want to make sure we never ask for anything that does not automatically carry invincible protection.

I sit in stillness,
Given the chance to be.
Quieting all thought,
I can clearly see…

A tiny little doorway,
Opening to me now.
Within it all the universe,
So, all I've become I allow.

Trying it on for size now,
Oh, how I love it so.
It fits like the perfect glove,
But this I already know.

I think I'll keep this glove on,
For all eternity.
Switching it up a bit now,
I embody the fullness of me.

What fun, and utter delight.
I remember why I am here.
Out on the leading edge of thought,
My dreams now instantly appear.

The path of least resistance only seems hard because we've been told our whole lives the good things in life are meant to be struggled for and that we are lazy and ungrateful if we take time to rest and recuperate.

The beauty of the "I AM Presence" is that it gives us an opportunity for the life of our dreams to manifest, and it will even work everything out for us if we surrender to the process. Most times this includes losing things like relationships, jobs, and items that may no longer be serving us.

As you expand your consciousness to higher levels of light there are things, situations, and people that are no longer a match for your light. When this occurs, this "leveling up" to higher light quotients, new things, situations, and people enter your life. The universe always has a much grander vision for you than you do. This is why surrendering to your "I AM Presence" is so very important.

But remember, surrendering to your "I AM Presence" is nothing more than surrendering to the highest aspect of yourself. Allowing yourself to see and embody this higher aspect of self gives you a knowing and a clear understanding: The one you are giving your control to is still you. It is the aspect of you that holds infinite divine wisdom, and it always has your best interest at heart because it is you and therefore, connecting and merging with it is important.

Do you know what fuels your desires,
And gives them their chance to be?
Why it is always the love,
Poured forth to your "I AM Presence,"
And that is always me.

I AM your Source,
For All That Is,
And I have always been.
I wait, and I wait, and I wait,
Until you turn within.

And as you send your love
To me, with dreams,
Desires, and wishes too...
That is the exact love,
I charge, and then return to you.

With the fulfillment
Of your call,
Yes, each and every one,
Blessed with the love you give,
Returned from the Great Central Sun.

So, turn inward now,
My beloveds,
And soon set yourself free,
I sit and wait just for you,
For all eternity.

There are seven laws of the universe dictating manifestation and the ways we connect and interact with our "I AM Presence", The Divine. They are called The Seven Principles of Correspondence (and can be researched more deeply by seeking Hermeticism, The Seven Hermetic Principles, or *The Kybalion*). They apply to everything and everyone.

1. Principle of Mentalism

This is the principle of the one mind. You can think of it as the principle of thought. It reminds you how powerful your thoughts are because they create your whole reality. If you want more good (thoughts/things) to show up in your life, think higher thoughts with their essence rooted in love.

2. Principle of Correspondence

This is the principle of *as above, so below, as within, so without.* Everything is a reflection of itself; your thoughts, feelings, emotions, vibration, rhythm, and energy inside of you is reflected outside of you. Absolutely everything you see and experience is a reflection from within. If something on the outside feels bad or unaligned, try identifying its source from within.

3. Principle of Vibration

What is vibration? It is an energy emittance from everything in existence. Everything has a vibrational frequency. It can be slow and dense, heavy and dark, or light and quick. Often, the energy you emit is a reflection of the vibration around you and vice versa. You can change your life and situation by emitting a higher vibration or surrounding yourself with the vibration you'd like to embody.

4. Principle of Rhythm

There is a rhythm to life. Just like the seasons, nothing in your life will stay exactly the same as it is now but will cycle through as things unfold and come into awareness. So, if something is perceived by you as bad in your life, it will not always be that way. Nothing is permanent in the physical sense. When you can embrace that, you allow the mind to flow and shift, like the seasons. You allow yourself to blow like the wind and find ease in the journey.

5. Principle of Polarity

Polarity is everywhere. Another word for polarity is *division*, but polarity can be a great gift. When you see something that instigates trouble or you label it as "bad," it is in fact the inspiration to evolve and to grow into something new. Look at what is present and allow yourself to see it in a new light. This propels you to a new perspective. It can be an energy to propel you for change.

6. Principle of Cause and Effect

What you do has an effect. If you take inspired action through your "I AM Presence," you are more likely to have a long-term positive effect than trying to go about things in separation consciousness. By activating intentions and actions that serve your highest good, positive effects and rewards come through.

7. Principle of Gender

Everything has masculine and feminine principles, gender manifests on all planes of existence. The universe is constantly seeking a balance of masculine and feminine energies. The existence of these energies in tandem is divine perfection. It is only through the lack of understanding, through thought and feeling, that humankind interrupts pure balanced flow. (Summarized/adapted after years of studying various resources as well as help from Source.)

If left uninterrupted, the essence of life would naturally express its perfection everywhere, and because everything is of the Divine Source, that means the ways in which masculine and feminine energies show up is also divine perfection. When humans are not in acceptance of divine perfection—however it shows up—there will be resistance because of the push back to the natural flow of the universe. Therefore, it is always best to be in full acceptance of what is, however life is choosing to show up. This means not trying to change it but allowing it to be what it is at any moment.

Absolutely everything is Source. Source is perfection. When you push against divine perfection, you will feel it. It's important to remember that however anything shows up, whenever it chooses to show up, it is perfect. It is God. We don't complain about it; we pour our love and offer it our full acceptance. When we do this, we can not only move through whatever is occurring with ease and grace, but we also become aware of the lesson—the gift of why it showed up the way it did.

The natural tendency of everything under The Divine is love, peace, harmony, beauty, and abundance. Life does not care who uses it, it seeks to pour more of its perfection into manifestation. The "I AM" is the activity of life and can be further provoked through speech. Many do not understand the laws of the universe, and, because of this, they speak such powerful words and draw forth into their experience things they may or may not wish to manifest.

They say, "Oh, I would have never asked for that." But you see, they did.

When you awaken to the truth of who you are at your core essence, you take full responsibility for your creations. You are the only one who can create for you. Therefore, everything you have experienced has been brought forth by you with divine perfection, whether you are aware of this or not.

You may not have been aware your words were powerful. When using your words in certain ways, especially when utilizing "I AM," it brings forth manifestation with whatever you connect to it. When you use the words "I AM," you are utilizing the full activity of God, and it is instantaneous in its action. All the powers of the entire universe then go into effect to produce that which you have intended with the use of "I AM" whether you have used the phrase consciously or unconsciously. With the conscious use of the "I AM," a clear understanding of whatever comes after those words will manifest into your reality.

TAKEAWAYS FOR YOUR TOOLBOX

When you think of the expression "I AM," it means you know you have God in action being expressed in your life. There are only two activities in life, and if you will not allow your inner "Mighty I AM Presence" to govern according to its plan of divine perfection, then the outer self—the ego—must do it. You can see how the collective of humanity has gotten itself into many unfortunate predicaments— even war—by allowing the outer self to lead the way.

When you fully accept your "I AM" as the Mighty Presence of God in you, you have taken one of the greatest steps to your liberation and freedom.

Always remember that God, your "I AM Presence," is the giver, the receiver, and the gift, and is the sole owner of all intelligence, substance, energy, and opulence there is in the whole universe. If one were to give God full credit for everything and all as they go about their life, such unbelievable transformations couldn't help but take place for the one who is giving full credit and power where it truly belongs.

You are each on your own unique journeys; therefore, no one can ever know what is best for you, except you. All the answers you could ever seek dwell within you now, within the "I AM Presence" you are one with. The whole universe is tucked away within you.

Meditation can be of great assistance in stilling your mind so you may hear your own inner voice. You can try placing your hand on your heart and asking your own "I AM Presence" any questions you may have while having no expectations or attachments to the outcome. Then, go about your day and the answer will come to you when it is divinely perfect for it to do so. It is all about trusting the divine process.

**Affirmations to Assist in Connecting and Merging with
Your "Mighty I AM Presence"**

I AM intending, commanding, and demanding, I AM the *Victory* of the great opulence of God made visible in my use right now, continuously, and for all eternity itself sustained; so be it, and so it is.

I AM intending, commanding, and demanding, I AM the *Victory* of the oneness and the consciousness and the pure knowing there is but one presence, one intelligence, and one power acting in my outer self, all my conditions, all my activities, and in my whole world and is my "Mighty I AM Presence," so be it, and so it is.

I AM intending, commanding, and demanding, I AM the *Victory* of demanding the silence of my outer self, and I AM intending, commanding, and demanding my outer self give its full obedience to my "Mighty I AM Presence," the highest divine aspect of who it is I AM now, continuously and for all eternity itself sustained; so be it, and so it is.

I AM intending, commanding, and demanding, I AM the *Victory* of fully acknowledging and joyously accepting my Mighty God Within, my Pure Christ, as the only Presence acting in my outer self, all my conditions, in all my activities, and in my whole world, now and for all eternity itself sustained; so be it, and so it is.

I AM intending, commanding, and demanding, I AM the *Victory* of having full faith, trust, and belief in the divine process and in the divine plan, that I AM one with now and for all eternity itself sustained; so be it, and so it is.

I AM commanding, demanding, and intending, I AM the *Victory* of always choosing to be divinely guided by my "Beloved I AM Presence," the highest divine aspect of who it is that I AM.

I AM intending, commanding, and demanding, I AM the *Victory of the oneness, the consciousness, and the knowing that I AM* right where I am meant to be, in this now moment and at any given moment, because all is always in divine perfect time and order; so be it, and so it is.

I AM intending, commanding, and demanding, I AM always the *Victory* of standing in all my power, speaking all my truth, and setting crystal clear boundaries for myself, now and for all eternity itself sustained: so be it, and so it is.

Chapter Two

Visitors from Beyond the Veil

here is a truth I have come to believe and know based upon my own experience. The truth is *love is always in command.* Love is the pure essence of All There Is, and love is who I AM, and it is who you are, too, at your core essence.

Sometimes the Universe, Source, God, Creator, your "Mighty I AM Presence"—whatever term you are comfortable with in describing who it is that created you and All That Is—can sometimes shake you out of your deep slumber to put you right where you need to be on your path in order to fulfill your soul's purpose. This is always for your highest good, even if you cannot recognize it as such at the time of its occurrence.

If you are unaware of who you truly are, and you have a specific divine purpose and a timeline for that specific divine purpose, the universe can, and oftentimes will, allow you to experience an event so life-changing you have no choice but to awaken to the truth of who you are. This is so you become fully aligned with your purpose.

As I journeyed further into my awakening process, inexplicable things started showing up. My husband and I decided to separate, so I moved into a relative's house with my son. While there, I noticed orbs appearing whenever I would take pictures, and they would also sometimes sparkle at the edge of my vision. It was a playful thing my son and I found great amusement in. As we explored further, my son and I realized that when we looked through our camera phones, we could see orbs easier than we could with the naked eye.

We had come to understand (from our research online), these orbs were The Divine in their nonphysical form. In other words, they were spirits existing without a physical body.

We found this fascinating; however, we were newbies to all things spiritual, and we were unaware there are spirits that are *not so much* of the light, meaning they are not embodying their true essence of the love they truly are, and instead are trapped in the ego mind.

I found myself at the end of a long day of wrapping Christmas gifts, lying on my bed resting. It was early evening, and my son was with me, standing at the foot of my bed. To give ourselves a break and a bit of fun, I opened my camera on the phone and started looking around the room for the orbs which had become so commonplace.

There were an exceptional number of orbs flying around in my bedroom that evening and my son and I were fascinated.

"Hold still. There are a few floating around you right now," I said to my son as I continued to capture them.

"How many?" he asked.

I flipped my phone so he could see.

"Woah! That's way more than we usually see in here. I wonder what they're doing?"

About five minutes into filming, my son let out a scream. He stood there with a look of panic on his face, glancing at his arm.

"What happened?" I asked, dropping my phone and jumping out of bed to check on him.

He held out his arm to me, and I saw three long scratches on his forearm like he'd been clawed by sharp fingernails. They were red and angry-looking, and I decided that it wasn't a good idea to continue filming, so I turned off the camera.

My son was visibly upset, but I wanted to be strong for him. I guided him to bed and settled down for the night, deciding it was best to take a break from spirit for a little while. I didn't really understand what I was doing by inviting them around, and I knew I was in unfamiliar territory. I decided to take a break for a bit in the filming of these orbs.

After a couple of hours had passed, I rolled over. With my eyes still closed I saw the faces of two old men flash in front of me. They looked grouchy and mean, and I had this intuitive feeling they were not the friendliest spirits. Putting two and two together, I knew they were likely responsible for the scratches on my son's arm.

I had a hard time falling asleep that evening. Not only was I a little spooked, but I could not get comfortable no matter what position I was in. After seeing those men's faces, my whole being was restless.

After barely sleeping a wink, I woke up early the next day. When I went to get out of bed, I found myself paralyzed. I had my full awareness and my wits about me, but I couldn't move from the bed. It was like the stickiest glue had dried and locked me to my mattress.

As the panic rose, I took a breath and decided to test my body. *Move your finger. Come on,* I urged myself, but it wouldn't budge. *Maybe my legs?* I tried again, but I could only breathe and think. Even my mouth was stuck, unmoving. I couldn't speak.

I took another breath and shut my eyes. *God, if you can hear me, I need you to help me now! What's going on? I need to get up! Help me now!* I prayed, and like a miracle, the weight on my body was lifted and I scrambled to get off the bed before the privilege was revoked. My body still felt stiff and hard to maneuver, but I rushed to the door and tried to open it.

Just like my body had been, the doorknob would not move. I prayed again, *God! Help me!*

Once again, as soon as I prayed and asked for help, I was able to open the door.

Out in the hallway, I did my best to walk to the stairs at the end of the hall. Halfway down, I was pushed back by a huge force nearly knocking me down in my weakened state.

Deciding I couldn't risk it, I continued to pray to God all the way down the hall. I was both petrified and angry my body wasn't working the way I wanted it to, and something was clearly preventing me from getting where I wanted to go. *I have no idea what is happening, but I am going to survive this, which includes getting the heck out of here in one piece,* I thought.

Through my stream of prayer, I was able to make it to the top of the stairs. I knew we had to leave. I screamed for my son as I descended the stairs, urging my body to keep moving, lest I got stuck again.

I heard him rush down the stairs to meet me, and I was instantly relieved he wasn't having the same problems I was that morning.

"What?" he asked, looking panicked.

I asked him to go find my phone and meet me promptly in the basement.

He nodded and went on his way, as I turned to make my way into the basement. I would have left the house immediately, but I wanted to be sure I took all my things before I fled. I wanted some privacy and to get away from whatever *that* was infesting the upper areas of the house.

When my son rejoined me, I grabbed him and flew down the steps to the basement.

"Mom, what's going on? What's wrong?"

I took my phone from him. "I don't know. I woke up and couldn't move my body, I'll explain it all on the way. Let's get out of here first," I said, realizing it'd be easier to tell him in the car than when we were basically running for our lives.

I clicked the buttons on my phone, trying to get the screen to light up, but the darn thing wasn't working. As it began to wake up, the screen would light up and then scramble, acting like it'd been dropped, or the screen had broken. I took a deep breath and started up my prayer mantra to find my phone finally working right.

I managed to look up and call a company that specialized in the paranormal. I knew of them from some of my spiritual research, but I had no idea their information would end up becoming useful to me until then.

"Hello?" a man answered on the other end of the line.

"Yes, hi! Thank God! I have a problem—"

Eagerly, the man on the other end interrupted me, "You need paranormal services? We can be out right away. Just let me know the address—"

"No, well, I don't think that'll work," I interrupted. "You see, this isn't my house, and I don't believe the owners will understand or appreciate the need for your services at this time. Though, I will say they are desperately needed. I am mostly calling because my son and I are holed up in the basement and I'm not entirely sure what to do next."

The patient man listened to me recount the events from the moment my son was scratched the night before, and he offered some advice.

"Sounds like the best thing you can do is get out of there and regroup. I believe it'll be safe for you to collect your things, but if anything happens in the meantime, you know how to get ahold of me, and by the way, Archangel Michael is the protector angel, and you can always call upon him for protection in times of trouble."

I thanked him and hung up.

"All right," I said to my son. "We're gonna need to speed pack. Grab everything you have and stick it down by the front door. We'll load the car from there."

"Where are we gonna go?" he asked.

That was a valid question. I hadn't really thought that far ahead, I assumed I'd figure it out once we'd left; I didn't want to spend any more time in the house with these angry spirits.

"We'll figure it out on the move, okay? For now, let's get our stuff and get outta here."

I gathered our belongings quickly, and my son and I jumped into my car. It was a cold, wintery day. I wanted to leave as quickly as possible and found myself wondering where we were going to go.

As I was driving, I made the decision to go to a hotel in town. Then, shortly after that, I had the idea to call my aunt.

"Hello?" she answered.

"Hello, it's Kim. Hi, so, there was an incident. I don't know what to say besides a lot of strange things happened to me this morning. We left in a huge hurry, but now we don't have anywhere to go. We were going to go to a hotel, but I need to talk to someone about this."

"Come on over. You know you're always welcome here," she said.

I didn't know if she actually believed me about what I had described to her but having a safe place to go with my son was enough for me.

Even though it was safe at my aunt's, I found the experience so traumatizing, and I was so afraid it would happen again, I didn't sleep for days.

Lying in my cousin's bed, I looked around the room. My cousin had a young son, and he had several pieces of his artwork hung around the room. In big, unsteady letters, *Michael* was scrawled in the corner of each piece.

Looking at that name, I felt a deep peace and comfort. With each piece and mention of my little cousin's name, I felt calmer. I remembered what the paranormal expert told me when I was on the phone with him.

He had asked me if I was familiar with Archangel Michael, the angel of protection. He said I could call upon the angel at any time. If I was ever in any type of crisis, Archangel Michael would be there to assist me. I somehow knew seeing the name Michael around the room was a sign for me from Archangel Michael himself, and he was present with me and my son and watching over the both of us and our safety.

After that traumatic event, I began to read more, and I searched even deeper to understand the meaning of what was occurring in my life. I came to understand sometimes the gentle signs and nudges aren't enough to help someone make the big changes they need to in life. Though it was scary, I know I wouldn't have begun the journey I was meant to be on without it. Everything is divine perfection, after all.

Unless asked, I didn't often talk to anyone except my son about the odd occurrences in my life. I knew my loved ones likely had some idea that things were out of the ordinary, especially since I wasn't my normal self, but I wasn't privy to whatever theories they had of this time in my life.

Whatever the path was, it was clearly mine to experience and move through, I had signs to let me know I was going in the right direction, and I knew that I was being watched over by the divine.

Divine time and order you say?
Oh how, oh how, can it be that way?
Some things happen that I can't believe,
And some things happened that I didn't ask to receive.

Can someone tell me how this can be?
Can someone please explain this to me?
Hello my child, I understand,
I am right here now, holding your hand.

There is a reason for all,
And this is true.
There are no coincidences,
Between me and you.

All, my dear one, is as it should be.
There is a much, much higher perspective you see.
All occurs for your growth in love and wisdom,
In becoming that which you already are...
My magnificent one, my child, my shining star!

I know for now, this may be difficult for you,
But, my dear one, I have a plan, it's true.
I ask you to trust now that my eyes can see.
I ask for you to believe in me.

I ask for you to relax,
And allow me to lead the way.
I ask for you to surrender to me this day.
All is well.
I love you.

Even though I could speak to my son about these things, I did not want to overwhelm him. He was only thirteen, and these happenings were as bizarre to him as they were to me.

One evening, my cousin had put her son to bed, and my aunt and uncle had retired for the evening. My cousin and I were relaxing and having a chat in the living room area, and it was the holiday season. My aunt had the most beautiful Christmas tree lit up in her formal living area, and I could see it from my place on the couch.

In otherwise complete darkness, the only light came from the television and the tree.

My cousin asked, "So, what do you think about mediums?"

I shrugged. "Never been to one before. Have you?"

Nodding, she said, "I went to visit one for fun a little while back."

I thought about it for a minute. The topic of spirituality was always on my mind now that I had many questions. Knowing my cousin was open to even speaking about unexplainable things was a comfort.

I told my cousin about my experience with Aunt Sallie after her funeral and reminded her of the crazy situation that led me to stay at her mom's.

"You think Aunt Sallie came back from the grave to sock ya in the arm? I guess that would be something she'd do."

I laughed, "That's what I—"

I paused and my eyes went wide. Across the house in the formal living room, I saw little red and white points of light floating around the tree. If I didn't see them floating around in midair, I would have thought they were Christmas lights.

As I watched, one of them grew and took form into a magnificent translucent being of light. It was faceless and had no truly discerning features besides the glowing white light of its lungs in its chest. It was made completely of sparkling white light and appeared almost like a fine mist. I could see the shape of the translucent figure being outlined in white light and it had a particular height.

The light being glided into the room.

"Are you seeing this?" I asked my cousin without looking away.

My cousin followed my gaze. "No, what is it? It feels like static electricity in here all of a sudden."

I explained to her what I was seeing so she could get a better sense of what she was feeling. Of course, I was disappointed she couldn't see it with me, and then that feeling quickly vanished.

The being stood directly in front of me and extended its hand, palm up, as if it were offering me something.

As soon as the first being formed, the other orbs formed into light beings and moved into the room with me and my cousin. Each walked as if it were gliding over the carpet. Their movements were graceful, and by their energy, I could tell they were excited. There were at least a couple dozen of them, and each one walked into the room and paused to look at me, emanating a feeling of peace and pure, unconditional love.

"What is this?" my cousin asked, feeling the growing static from the increase of energetic light beings in the room.

I was astounded. "I have no idea, but this is beautiful. What do you think we should do?"

"Hmm, maybe ask them to go back into the other room and we can call them back by name? You must know who they are if you can see them, right?"

I looked at her and then at the individual, faceless light beings around us. She was right, I knew them, and so did she. Although they were faceless, I intuitively knew they were my family. I felt they had come to show their love and support for the recent events I had experienced, and I was grateful my cousin was also there to witness it.

"Okay, everyone. Please return to the other room, and we will call you in to greet you one at a time."

As if on cue, the beings of light turned and gracefully moved back into the other room for us.

"Mom, please come forward," I said, feeling nervous and elated to experience my mother's presence after decades of missing her.

The first light being—the one who'd come into the room and offered me its hand—moved back into the room to stand in front of me once more and reached out her hand for me to grab.

While the beings didn't have any defining gender, I recognized this one as being the same height I remembered as my mom's, and the gentleness of her touch was of my mother's, as her spiritual hand sent energetic pins and needles into my own. She even had the same calm personality.

"My mom is here," I said, keeping my cousin in the loop on what was happening. I glanced at my cousin and saw tears streaming down her face.

Through quiet sobs, she asked, "Can I have a hug from her?"

Hearing her request, my mother moved from me to my cousin and leaned over to hug her.

"She's hugging you," I informed her, and she laughed nervously.

"I can feel pins and needles!"

I took a deep breath as my mother's figure moved around the sofa to wait in the kitchen. Turning back to the waiting light beings, I called in my grandmother next, then Aunt Sallie and others.

As each light being was called, they walked—glided—forward and extended a hand to me.

"Who's next?" I asked.

"Have you called Uncle Eddie yet?"

I shook my head. "Okay, Uncle Eddie. Please come forward."

As the being identified as Uncle Eddie floated forward, I noticed he was tall and had a feature the other beings didn't have.

"He has a heart!" I told my cousin.

"What do you mean?"

"Like, a heart in his chest. It's right there and it's bright purple!"

"What does that mean?"

I shrugged as he extended his hand to me. Having gotten used to the feeling of pins and needles, and enjoying getting to touch my loved ones again, I placed my hand on top of his.

There was so much love in the room, my cousin and I couldn't hold back our tears of love and appreciation in return. We were excited, too. The parade of my family members was such a blessing, it felt like a celebration.

When I called my sister, she came right into the room. We greeted each other immediately. She was still the height of a child, as she was when she'd passed, and we were nearly eye-to-eye from where I was seated on the couch.

She extended one hand to me, and I took it happily. She passed away when I was a toddler, so I'd never known her as well as some of the other relatives there. Still, I loved her and welcomed her.

If I had to guess, about thirty beings of light came to us that evening. As we came down to the end of our list of names, I started asking my cousin for more names, as I couldn't remember who I might be forgetting.

She also struggled to remember any others, but I realized there might be others besides our family there.

I'd read once that sometimes spirit guides can appear for us in that same way, so I decided to call upon mine. "If there are any of my spirit guides present, please show yourselves and come forward. I am eager to meet you!"

A being who acted more energetic than the others appeared and strutted into the room. I got the feeling he was more masculine in nature, and although he was quite short, he was brimming with confidence. Though spirit has no gender, I intuitively knew he must have been a male in another lifetime when I knew him.

Spirit guides are benevolent beings of light assigned to you for a specific lifetime, and they assist you in navigating your life's journey. They are always present with you, and if you ask for their help, and intend for it, you will receive it. While we are each blessed with free will, The Divine will intervene in our lives if called upon to do so. We must first ask for help for it to be given, and my guide reflected that.

I giggled. He was filled with positive energy, and he extended his two hands to me, not one hand like all the others previously. It was so nice to meet one of my guides. I felt he was also excited to meet me. It was truly an amazing experience.

My cousin and I were so exuberant and excited by our visitation, we didn't notice we were being loud. My aunt came down the stairs.

"Why are you all so noisy down here? What are you girls doing up so late? It's one o'clock in the morning!" she informed us.

"The most amazing things have been happening! You'll never believe it," my cousin said.

My aunt walked into the living room and sat down next to my cousin on the sofa. I had been standing and greeting the light beings as they entered the room, and suddenly, with my aunt's arrival, I was feeling a little exposed. I also had no idea it had gotten so late.

We each did our best to explain to her what had happened, but I could tell none of it was really landing. My aunt wasn't really into the spiritual, and she seemed closed off to the new information. However, I was feeling the exact opposite. Even though I had been through a traumatic experience, this new encounter with my loved ones from the other side of the veil renewed my excitement and curiosity.

After we'd finished explaining what had happened, my aunt took a deep breath. She looked tired.

"All right, I won't pretend to understand anything you said, but I can say it's time to wrap it up and head to bed now. Any more of this and you'll wake up the rest of the house."

As she spoke, I watched as the spirit of my mother reappeared beside my aunt. She leaned down and hugged her, and I smiled, eager to see if she felt the same pins and needles my cousin and I had.

"Your sister is leaning down and hugging you! Can you feel her?" I asked my aunt.

"Oh, Kim," she scoffed, getting up from the sofa, "that's ridiculous. There's no way she's here—let alone somehow touching me. It's a lovely sentiment, but I can't believe it."

My mother stood and moved back into the kitchen once my aunt voiced her opinion, and I felt a little crushed. I know there's no way to force people to see and believe in The Divine, but it would have been nice to have my aunt be open to the possibility.

"Now, it's late and I'm tired. You two head on up to bed, okay?"

I sighed, not wanting to leave the light beings, my family, yet. "You guys go ahead. I'm going to lie on the couch for a while."

They agreed and left me to my own devices for the evening so I could settle into the knowing I had experienced family I'd considered to be completely gone at one point or another in my life.

As I lay on the sofa after saying my farewells to my relatives from the other side of the veil, one last light being glided into the room.

I looked at the being and said, "I appreciate your presence, but I am exhausted after all that. I'm going to be resting now, okay?"

The light being glided even closer, even after hearing my plea for rest, and sat down next to me on the sofa.

I sighed. "All right, you're welcome to sit there as long as you'd like, but you should know I'll probably be falling asleep soon."

Georgie.

As clear as day, the name rang through my mind. I'd like to say I was prepared, but I still couldn't believe any of it.

Georgie was Aunt Sallie's son. He'd passed away shortly after Aunt Sallie did, and he wasn't much older than me.

We'd called every family member we could think of who'd passed on, but I realized we'd forgotten to call Georgie. I felt so upset for forgetting him.

"Oh, Georgie! I'm so sorry I forgot to call on you. Stay as long as you want to, okay? I love you," I said.

I knew the light being was pure unconditional love and acceptance; however, I still felt terrible for having forgotten to call upon him and wanted Georgie to feel appreciated and included. He accepted my offer to stay, and I fell asleep soon after.

The following morning, as we gathered around the breakfast table, my cousin and I were still abuzz with the events of the previous evening.

We filled my uncle in on what had happened, and I told him what the light beings looked like.

"They were all different heights, like they would have been when I knew them in life, and I could see their lungs so clearly even though they were translucent. But one of them had more. I saw a bright purple heart in his chest."

My uncle grunted. "That's interesting. You know your uncle recieved a Purple Heart during the war."

My cousin and I exchanged a look. "You mean Uncle Eddie?" I asked.

"Yes. He was a Seabee in Guam during World War II. He helped build the airport runway there as far as I can remember," my uncle explained.

I couldn't believe it. While I knew the light being with the purple heart was my Uncle Eddie, I couldn't believe it was being confirmed to me over breakfast. The experience with my family was real and it was special. They wanted me to know who they were, and they wanted me to know they were there to support me.

This is the unfamiliar,
The never have been before.
Yet, also familiar,
Quite strange to be sure.

Alas, onward you go,
Expanding in each now.
The surrender to divinity,
You do so allow.

For you know, you are never alone…
And you have never been.
The whole universe tucked away,
Magnificently within.

How absolutely amazing,
Beyond which these words can reveal,
For they are merely fool's gold,
To the diamond of how you feel.

TAKEAWAYS FOR YOUR TOOLBOX

It is true our family members never leave us. The entire universe is pure love energy, and our loved ones who transition, never truly go away; they change form. They are ever present with us, guiding and supporting us, through pure, unconditional love, and light at all times.

I have come to know this as my own truth from my experiences. My family's visitation immediately put me at ease and brought peace when I needed it most.

With your pure intent, you can call upon your own family of light at any time for divine support. This is exactly what I did, and support showed up in droves. There is always infinite divine support available to you at any given moment. It is an ask away.

We each have free will. It is because of this free will, and an agreement that has been put into place by us; The Divine will not intervene on our behalf unless we ask and intend for it to do so.

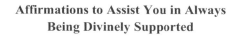

Affirmations to Assist You in Always Being Divinely Supported

I AM commanding, demanding, and intending, I AM the *Victory* of choosing to always be divinely guided, assisted, supported, healed, helped, and loved unconditionally beyond measure; so be it, and so it is.

I AM commanding, demanding, and intending, I AM the *Victory* of being one now with the consciousness and the pure knowing that The Divine always has my back, at any given moment, now, continuously, and for all eternity itself sustained; so be it, and so it is.

I AM commanding, demanding, and intending, I AM always the *Victory* of choosing to be nourished, nurtured, cared for, and comforted by The Divine; so be it, and so it is.

I AM commanding, demanding, and intending, I AM the *Victory* of always being infinitely divinely blessed and provided for by The Divine now, continuously, and for all eternity itself sustained; so be it, and so it is.

I AM commanding, demanding, and intending, I AM the *Victory* of surrendering now and always, absolutely everything, and all to The Divine, to my own "I AM Presence," for my highest good and for the highest good of all; so be it, and so it is.

Chapter Three

Community

uring our next relocation, my son and I chose to stay at an extended stay hotel, that happened to be near a Victorian house that had been converted into a holistic store. Soulutions for Daily Living became a haven for me as I navigated the spiritual awakening I was experiencing.

There were several parts to Soulutions, and Honey, the owner, oversaw it all. When I first met her, she was at the register, warm and welcoming. It felt like I'd known her all my life.

"Welcome to Soulutions. What can I help you with?" she asked.

I took a deep breath, and a fragrant aroma in the shop filled my lungs. It calmed me instantly. "There's quite a bit you can help me with, but I don't know if you have the time to hear it all."

Honey smiled. "I have all the time in the world right now. Tell me what's going on."

Maybe it was her calm demeanor or her groundedness, I'm not sure, but I knew I could trust her, and she would do her best for me. So, I told her everything.

Once Honey had heard my plight and knew what I'd been dealing with practically on my own, she nodded. "That's quite a bit. Sounds like you've been experiencing the beginning of your ascension process."

I looked at her questioningly. I'd never heard the term *ascension* before. I asked her to clarify.

She led me to a section of the store where I could find the information.

"If you want," she said, "there's an area on that side of the store where you can sit and read for a while to be sure you're getting the right book. While I'm certain whatever you're led to pick up will be divinely perfect for you, it never hurts to browse before leaving the store with something."

I thanked her and spent several hours in Soulutions. As inexplicable as everything else in my life, finding her store was a lifesaver for me, and spending time there felt like home.

I began cultivating my new spiritual community through Honey and my time at Soulutions shortly after.

As I found more peace for my life through the wealth of information I gathered and the skills I cultivated at the store, I found it was much easier to make decisions. After a short stint at the hotel, I decided it was time to find a more permanent place for my family and started looking for an apartment. The Divine was right by my side and guided the way the entire time.

Chance happenings,
I think not.
For divine time,
Is all we've got.

It is right here.
It is right now.
There is no other way,
There is no other how.

The book that magically,
Comes your way,
And on that page,
Knows just what to say,

To lift your heart,
Into eternal bliss,
To remind you once again,
That naught is amiss.

Or that person,
That sits right next to you,
Who sees a twinkle in your eye,
And asks, "What is it you do?"

All opportunities they are,
To see what's already there,
The love we all are,
We are remembering to share.

No, there are no coincidences,
No accidents, you can be sure.
Love orchestrates all,
And only love will endure.

One apartment my son and I visited was a couple towns over and it seemed all right at first look, but the signs that followed proved otherwise.

When we were driving home from viewing the apartment, we stopped at a traffic light, and as we were waiting for it to change, we were chatting about what we liked and disliked about the apartment.

On the other side of the street, on the passenger side of my car, there was a raised parking lot with a guardrail to prevent cars from driving off the massive drop-off and onto the street.

Out of the corner of my eye, I caught movement and noticed a car barrel through the guardrail of the parking lot heading straight for the side of the car where my son was seated. We both gasped, but there was nowhere I could move the car to make sure it would miss us. The light was still red, and I couldn't reverse in time to get out of the way.

In a split second, almost like a time shift, the flying car pivoted midair, and flew behind us, missing our back bumper by mere inches.

"Are you okay?!" I shouted at my son, reaching out in a panic. "Did you see that?"

Looking as shocked as I felt, he nodded. "Yeah."

I looked in the rearview mirror and had to take a minute to compose myself. I thought to myself, *There was no way that wasn't a warning.* I interpreted our near-miss accident as a sign we needed to look for an apartment somewhere completely different from the apartment we'd just seen.

To seek answers for life in general as well as new places to look for apartments, I often turned to the oracle cards Honey left out for patrons. Like many of the tools I received while walking my spiritual path, oracle cards were simple, accurate ways to receive divine wisdom and guidance using my intention.

I learned much of what I knew about oracle cards from the many mediums, intuitives, and shamans who came to visit the store or to meet with their clients for readings. Every time I went to Soulutions, I treated it like a class I could learn from, and that outlook never ceased to teach me something new and helped me gain a deeper insight into my own divinity. Oracle cards are a divination tool one can utilize to gain a deeper understanding of *what is* for one's highest good at any given moment.

I became proficient at reading the oracle cards and sometimes I would even be asked for readings by patrons of Soulutions.

Gaining insight from my own intuition and with a little guidance from the oracle cards, I managed to find a beautiful apartment for my son and me that had everything we needed and were looking for in a home.

Another connection I made through the Soulutions community was with a visiting practitioner who utilized space at the store for his healing crystal bed. I had no idea what a crystal bed was, and I did a little research on it before it arrived. Honey assured me it would be a benefit to me and was convinced I'd like it. She opened a schedule for people to book sessions with the crystal bed healer, so I signed up.

When I got to my session, a soft-spoken man greeted me. "Is there anything ailing you at the moment?" he asked.

I thought about it for a moment. Since I was a young adult, I'd had a chronic condition I had to take medication for daily. I told him about it.

He nodded before explaining, "So, the way the crystal bed works is that someone in need of healing will lie down on the bed and rest under a giant copper pyramid suspended in the air. A chromotherapy machine uses crystals to filter spectrums of light into your crown chakra. Each color is thought to target a specific meridian or energy center in the body. Also, the session may involve some element of sound healing, visualization, or meditation. As the crystals light up, the colors help focus the energy of the chakra points to create a more cohesive energy flow within and without of the body."

I nodded. "So, the crystals are like energy beacons for your chakras?"

"Exactly," he said. "Energy therapy is one of many ways we can heal ourselves and better align with Source."

After my first session, I became fixated on learning the workings of the crystal bed and booked many sessions while it was at Soulutions. Some of my family and friends were also curious and came to have a session.

The fact they were open to exploring a small portion of the vast resources and community I'd come to know and love, meant a great deal to me at the time.

The man with the crystal bed also offered spiritual classes and private past-life readings and because I was a sponge for all information of a spiritual nature, I signed up for most everything offered. The most compelling of the classes he offered was an ascension course.

Though I'd learned plenty through the resources and books Honey had in the store, taking a class about spiritual ascension was another thing entirely. I was surprised to find the class nearly full when I arrived.

"Hello, everyone," the presenter greeted. "Before we start with the class, I want to preface by saying, if you're open to it, the information you will remember from this class and the energy you will receive and then integrate, will change your life. It's no secret

The Divine brings us places we never expected to be, but we are always better off for it, and this is no exception."

I took a deep breath, settling into his words. Of course, I knew what he was saying to be true, but the continued confirmation of it meant more to me than anything else. Each time I was reminded all is always in divine time and order and I AM right where I AM meant to be at any given moment. I knew The Divine was present with me.

There was safety in the wisdom I was about to remember. I say *remember* because we are not learning anything. We are already one with the infinite, divine wisdom that is tucked away within each of us. Therefore, it becomes a remembering, not a learning of anything, as you gain wisdom along your journey, helping you to reveal the truth of who it is you truly are.

The ascension process is one of spiritual awakening which shifts you into a higher state of consciousness. It is the process by which you merge back into the wholeness you have always been but have temporarily forgotten.

As the class continued, the instructor spoke on subjects I'd never heard of before. Topics like New Earth and Oneness were foreign to me up to that point. I took copious notes throughout the class to take into my future studies.

He also recounted his many etheric adventures and the mystery schools he experienced while exploring the higher states of consciousness. It was explained to me what personal ascension was and what it meant regarding myself and the human collective consciousness—how higher states of being could lift the whole of humanity, benefiting all.

The information from the class was detailed and thorough, and it gave me hope for the direction I was headed.

The ascension class was a three-day event. We were not only learning about ascension, but the presenter also facilitated energetic clearings for each of us to have an easier time of achieving the next level of our souls' journeys.

While I'd done plenty of work on the crystal bed, the full-body energetic clearing was another thing entirely. The work on the bed felt like an alignment whereas this felt like a releasing and removal of density I hadn't even realized was there.

"All right everyone, we're going to take our healing white light and imagine it moving into our throat area to clear out any discordant energy affecting our throat chakras," the presenter said. "Often the throat chakra can become blocked by feelings of voicelessness, a fear of speaking up or being heard, being bullied intentionally or unintentionally, negative self-talk, and believing your opinion is invalid or not worth voicing because it may stir things up and cause unnecessary drama. I want you to know your voices *do* matter, and you deserve to be seen and heard."

When I visualized the white light moving through my body and into my throat, I started coughing violently. While I tried willing myself to stop, I ended up interrupting the class for five minutes with the longest coughing fit of my life. I was definitely clearing something major in my throat chakra.

It was so strange because I hadn't really thought I wasn't being heard, and I wasn't identifying with any of the reasons why my throat chakra would be blocked. Turns out there was more there than I initially realized—possibly from a past life—and based on the coughing, my body was ready to release it.

Amazingly, I didn't truly know what a chakra was until the first day of ascension class, let alone know it was something that needed to be tended to on a regular basis. Through the teachings of the class, I can say the new ascension knowledge kick-started my *own* ascension process into high gear.

After class, everything began to shift for me on a grand scale. I began a major clearing process that would last several years. From that moment forward, I would spend much of my time clearing energies out of my field that weren't serving my highest good in co-creation with The Divine. The class taught me several techniques for clearing, and I was putting them to good use in all areas of my life. I was truly grateful for them.

Through my ascension class, I was also beginning to see evidence in my life that I was connecting to my soul family. This ascension class brought those of us together of a similar consciousness and allowed us to share our thoughts with each other that led to even more growth for me on a spiritual level.

Friends of near,
And friends from far...
Oh, what a divinely blessed,
Family we are.

Physical distance,
Means no thing.
For within time/no time,
I still hear your heart sing.

Even just a whisper,
Soothes my soul,
From ancient times,
We are one and whole.

Gather dear ones,
Of luminous, eternal light.
Dance to the sacred tune,
On this perfect, divine night.

We are one.

TAKEAWAYS FOR YOUR TOOLBOX

A soul family is comprised of a group of people your soul energetically resonates with on a physical, emotional, mental, and spiritual level. These beings are members of the same "spirit family" as you, and they share an intensely strong bond that transcends time and space itself. You more than likely have spent many previous lifetimes with these beings. You have a familiarity with them whether you have originated from the same star system or the same planet.

For example, you may resonate and connect with others in this incarnation whom you have spent lifetime after lifetime within Arcturus, Sirius, or possibly in the Pleiades. Therefore, you have a particularly strong bond with them.

As you journey on your ascension path, releasing what no longer serves you and embodying your own "I AM Presence," you allow for those connections to reemerge into your awareness and experience. This occurs because you all came here with a specific soul mission and to accomplish that mission, which is the divine plan fulfilled. You energetically are drawn to each other and group together, in order to have a more profound and positive effect on the evolution of the collective consciousness on the planet.

How does one find their soul family? Well, there is nothing to do except turn inward and continuously align your own inner compass with pure joy and pure unconditional love, your own "I AM Presence." This activity will put out a signal and draw those cooperating components into your life, which can take the form of other people, places, things, and situations to accomplish spec-ifically what you came here to achieve. Everything will line up for you when you align with your own "I AM Presence." This is the task at hand for all of us.

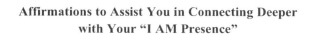

**Affirmations to Assist You in Connecting Deeper
with Your "I AM Presence"**

I AM commanding, demanding, and intending, I AM the *Victory* of being in my "I AM Presence," and my "I AM Presence" is in me; so be it, and so it is.

I AM commanding, demanding, and intending, I AM the *Victory* of the oneness and the consciousness and the pure knowing that what I AM seeking is also seeking me at any given moment, now, continuously, and for all eternity itself sustained; so be it, and so it is.

I AM the *Victory* of commanding, demanding, and intending as I allow myself to follow my own joy, I know everything and all aligns *for* me in perfect divine time and order; so be it, and so it is.

I AM commanding, demanding, and intending, I AM the *Victory* of being one with the consciousness and the knowing everything and all has already been created, and I AM choosing now to be the Victory of ever aligning with my highest timeline and my highest resonance and light; so be it, and so it is.

I AM commanding, demanding, and intending, I AM the *Victory* of always being aligned with my divine blueprint, my soul's mission; so be it, and so it is.

I AM commanding, demanding, and intending, I AM the *Victory* of always being one with Divine eternal peace within as well as with the pure knowing all is unfolding for me in divine perfect time and order, always for my highest good and for the highest good of all That I AM; so be it, and so it is.

I AM commanding, demanding, and intending, I AM the *Victory* of the oneness and the consciousness and the pure knowing as I become aware of all of the synchronicities in my life, more and more are occurring for me, always for my highest good and for the highest good of all; so be it, and so it is.

I AM commanding, demanding, and intending, there is only God, "The Mighty I AM Presence," acting everywhere present now; so be it, and so it is.

Chapter Four

Angels

*L*ove and acceptance are the keys to bringing forth the perfect divine solution for any disharmony. Before I became aware of loving and accepting all in one's experience and fully aligning with my "Mighty I AM Presence," I had experienced some imbalance in my life. I knew being a part of the new ascension class was having a positive effect on my being and my life overall. I made several new friends through the class, which opened new avenues to learn and grow my spiritual practice. Things were brighter.

I became fast friends with a woman in the class who I met the first day. We had many conversations, and she told me much about her own journey into spirituality.

One day, we were talking, and she said, "Kim, a good friend of mine is hosting a spiritual event at her home, and I think you need to come."

"What's it about?" I asked.

"She's invited someone who channels Archangel Raphael. I believe we get a chance to ask questions. I think it'll be fun."

"What do you mean by *channels*? What's channeling?" I asked.

She smiled. "There are lots of ways to do it, I guess, but in this instance, I believe the channeler allows The Divine to speak through her."

I hadn't thought much of communing with The Divine before, but the idea of channeling sounded right up my alley. "I'd love to come," I told her.

I had read about Archangel Raphael, and I knew the angel was the divine Archangel of Healing. I was interested to see how this could positively affect my life.

I told my son about the event, too, and he decided to come along. I believed the shared experience would be nice.

I was so excited as we pulled up to a beautiful home. Upon arriving, I saw my friend, and we all entered together. There were approximately fifteen people in attendance, and we all took our seats in a semicircle with the woman who channeled Archangel Raphael, Kelly Kolodney, taking her seat in front of us.

The host stepped up to the front of the room once we'd settled. "Hello everyone and thank you for coming. While I'm sure you all know why we're here, I'd like to take this moment to introduce Kelly Kolodney," she said, offering her a chance to speak.

Kelly smiled at the group before taking the floor. She spoke about herself and how she became a channeler before she introduced us to the concept of toning.

"Toning," she said, "is a way of aligning the body and spirit to those you wish to make a connection with. In my case, I sing-song in a way that allows for Archangel Raphael to merge with me and speak through me, enabling the angel's messages of love and wisdom to come forth for the highest good of all."

When she began toning, I paid close attention. The sounds were angelic, melodic, and beautiful, and it made the whole space feel lighter.

After a minute or so, there was a slight energy shift to Kelly's body and the angel spoke *through* her. It was fascinating to me, and I hung onto every word she said.

"Hello, hello, hello. We are pleased to see you all here. There is a lot of love in this room, and we are grateful for your participation." The angel laughed. "We have come to answer any questions you may have and are open to your inquiries. What is it?" the angel asked.

I raised my hand. The questions came to me like rapid fire.

Raphael motioned for me to speak, so I did. "Archangel Raphael, hello and thank you for being here, I would like to ask you why I am going through these particular experiences. And could you please explain the meaning of all of it?"

The angel hummed. "We all have a divine purpose, one of which is to love self and all as self. In addition to that, your specific purpose is of a spontaneous, direct healer. You are experiencing these divine occurrences so you may align with your soul's mission for this lifetime."

"What is a spontaneous, direct healer?"

The angel giggled a bit again. "You will heal others by seeing them as already whole. You will hold space, as a loving witness, allowing for a rebalancing of their energies to occur. You will help others to be in full acceptance of whatever may be showing up for them in their experience. Therefore, you will be assisting them to move through any perceived disharmony with ease."

"Will I be able to do this for everyone?" I asked.

"For those who choose it, yes. Sometimes a soul may decide it is their particular time to leave their physical vessel, and on a conscious level, they may not be aware of that decision. Therefore, in those instances, you will not be able to assist them in the healing of their physical form, but don't be alarmed. It is all divine perfection, and they are as much on their path as you are on yours." I thanked the angel who then turned to speak to another member of our gathering.

After the channeling event, I was on a mission, more than ever before, to discover myself more deeply. I began to question who I really was. At this channeling event, I found out some amazing information about myself I had not known before.

Archangel Raphael became a wonderful guide from that moment forward, and through the angel, I was introduced to other Great Ascended Masters of Light who continue to assist me in healing as well as all things having to do with my soul purpose, which is the divine plan fulfilled.

Trusting deeply,
Blindly I go.
The path ahead,
I do not know.

The mystery deep,
Within me now.
No more answers,
To when or how.

Hands outstretched,
To feel my way,
Light within,
Guides the way.

All is well,
In this tunnel, bright.
I journey now,
With only light.

My son and I made our move into a new apartment complex with the blessing from The Divine of a smooth journey. It was around this time I also began my one-on-one sessions with Kelly Kolodney who channeled the Archangel Raphael.

When I sat down with Kelly and the angel for the first time in a private setting, the message Source had for me was clear: eat, sleep, live, and breathe everything Archangel Michael.

"Kim, you are similar to a toddler at this stage," Archangel Raphael explained. "You are still finding your balance and learning how to walk in this world of spirit. Just as if you were building a house, we will need to start first with building a strong foundation, one that cannot be toppled. Your ascension is happening, but it is very important to go purposefully, step by step."

I nodded, understanding what the angel was saying.

The angel continued, "Also, at this time, your being is susceptible to discordant energies. It is similar to a newborn baby being left in the woods. Therefore, I suggest you work closely with Archangel Michael, the protector angel, in these early stages until you are better able to master your own energy field."

When Archangel Raphael spoke about Archangel Michael, I was immediately reminded of being at my aunt's house in my cousin's room and surrounded by her son Michael's artwork. It brought back the feeling of peace and security I'd felt in that space and how it had helped me sleep soundly for the first time in days since the incident with the orbs.

I did not know it then, but synchronicity was at play. I felt an immediate sense of calm come over me when I saw the name on the art that evening. I knew Archangel Michael was present with me.

I took a deep breath, knowing I was secure and protected. "How can I bring Archangel Michael more into my life?" I asked.

Archangel Raphael laughed in a light, loving, airy way. "We would like you to begin by immersing yourself in Archangel Michael's energy. Whatever reminds you of him you can keep around you and on your person. This is worth exploring and implementing at this time. We would like you to eat, sleep, and breathe all things Archangel Michael. It is for your highest good you take in as much information about him as possible. He is always ever present with you, but as you immerse yourself in his energy, even more so, it will allow him to become even closer to you. Anything you can do to bring him closer and immerse yourself in Archangel Michael's energy is important for you at this time."

I nodded, allowing myself to ponder what needed to be done in order to bring Michael's energy closer to me, and integrate it with my own.

"Archangel Michael will be focused on you and will be your protector throughout this time. Think of it as if you are a child entering school. No one would expect you to jump straight into writing your dissertation when you don't even know how to write your ABCs. Therefore, as you are similar to a child who cannot properly protect herself at this time, Archangel Michael will be there as backup for your protection while you learn."

I realized what Archangel Raphael was explaining sounded more like an infant who needed constant care. Based on my experience, I knew there was no way I could protect myself without the direct help of The Divine. And while that was unfamiliar, I was open to having the divine assistance in areas where I clearly couldn't take care of myself.

From the first time I heard Archangel Raphael speak, I intuitively felt what the angel was saying was true. I could feel it in my soul as it resonated with me immediately and deeply. I also knew how important it was for me to pay close attention to all the suggestions being made. I did my best and followed the advice as best as I could.

I decided to visit Soulutions, and I asked Honey if she had any books about Archangel Michael. It turned out Honey had *many* books on this powerful angel in stock.

I proceeded to purchase most of them and began my quest to find out as much as I could about Archangel Michael and immerse myself in his energy. During this time, I recognized and could feel divine Archangel Michael's presence always right by my side. After all I had experienced up until this point, I was comforted, relieved, and happy to know this was the case.

I take this moment,
To tell you true,
There is nothing more powerful,
Than the love within you.

No trials, tribulations,
Or darkness of night,
Can ever take hold,
Of your luminous light.

Oh, it can try,
But I tell you this,
It is nothing more,
Than a fleeting wish.

For the light of all creation,
You have always been.
To summon forth,
At your very whim.

So be courageous, be confident,
And shine with all your might.
This battle has already been won,
And the victor is the light.

One evening, as my son and I were about to go to sleep in our apartment, we had an unexpected visit. My son was lying in his bed, and I was sitting up in my bedroom reading a book.

Suddenly, a golden mass of what I can only describe as sparkles descended into my room followed by a second mass of white ones. They were each approximately eight to ten feet tall and about three feet in width. They hovered and oscillated in midair before me.

At the same time, my son happened to be making his way into my room. He asked me what was happening, and I pointed to the mass of sparkles in the center of my bedroom and explained that these divine guests, whoever they were, had arrived. I knew intuitively they were angels, and they were benevolent. I noticed it also became extremely cold in my room upon their arrival.

My son could feel the cold air, too, and he spontaneously jumped on top of my bed and placed his hand in the middle of one of the masses to see if he could feel anything. He said all he could feel was the cold air within the energy mass itself. My son then proceeded to explain the reason he had been on his way to my room.

He told me he had been lying on his bed with all his lights out, ready to fall asleep, when something made him look up at the ceiling. Just as he looked up, he said he saw the word *God* written, as plain as day, on his ceiling. He then told me he reached out his hands, doing his best to try and touch the word.

Unfortunately, he had no success as the word was on the ceiling. It was much too high for him to reach. It was then my son decided to come and tell me what had happened.

The angels stayed for what seemed like a long while, until my son and I got a bit tired and then they left. They did not speak; they were present with us. It was an amazing experience to see the angels in a lit room as their light was so bright, dazzling, and mesmerizing.

I feel this experience had several meanings for my son and me. On the one hand, it was allowing both my son and me to become more familiar with the unfamiliar. It was also a reassurance The Divine is benevolent and is always present with us whether we can perceive them with our senses or not.

It was yet another experience in our awakening processes. It served to open our awareness to the pure knowing we are never alone and never have been.

The angelic host always sees all of humanity in its divine perfection. It sees each human being as one with the Creator. The angelic host is available to all of humanity equally; it is not bound by any human limitation or belief. It takes your participation in calling upon and calling forth their love and light to assist you with your divine freedom of will.

Archangels and Their Expertise

The archangels serve the whole of humankind. When called upon from the heart with pure intention, they serve humanity with love, acceptance, and compassion. Some of their duties include the facilitation of life paths, soul contracts, order within the natural world, and more. They can also act as a bridge to help us receive divine inspiration and wisdom.

You can call upon them at any time, either aloud or to yourself, and you will be heard. You can also call upon your own "Beloved I AM Presence," who then uses divine messengers, some of which are the archangels, to carry out your intended request.

Even the names of The Divine are powerful and connected. All names with "el" in them, like Michael and Gabriel, mean "Those of God." Many of the angels are named with this connection to Source.

Listed below are a few of the archangels and their specific areas of expertise. With your intention, you can ask them for what you are desiring, aligning it always for the highest good of all and divine will.

Archangel Ariel–Lioness of God

Archangel Ariel oversees environmental causes and is known to be a guardian and healer of animals. She can also assist you in providing for your physical needs, such as shelter, money, and supplies.

Archangel Azrael–God Helps

Azrael lovingly guides departed souls to Heaven, back to Source. He also consoles the bereaved families and friends to assist them in healing from their grief.

Archangel Chamuel–He Who Sees God

The archangel's omniscient vision enables them to see the connection between everyone and everything. Archangel Chamuel can ease anxiety and bring about personal and even global peace. The archangel is also able to assist you in locating lost objects or anything you may be looking for. When asked with pure intent, this archangel can also assist in bringing harmony into all your relationships.

Archangel Gabriel–Messenger of God/God Is My Strength

Archangel Gabriel's ultimate gift is to pass along messages from God, the "I AM Presence." The archangel is closely aligned with child-rearing and pregnancy. This archangel is the herald of visions. Archangel Gabriel helps to make God's messages understandable to people for them to easily accept these messages with a pure heart.

Archangel Haniel–Glory of God

She is associated with Venus and the moon. Her gift is to empower spiritual practitioners to gain heightened intuition. Haniel also provides divine guidance to those who seek to develop their intuitive abilities.

Archangel Jeremiel–Mercy of God

Archangel Jeremiel's duty is to help souls review their life on Earth. The archangel does not pass judgment but is honest in order for people to learn and evolve. The archangel wants you to see the "light" of the situation so you can plan for positive change.

Archangel Jophiel–Beauty of God

This archangel is known as the patron of artists. The archangel can heal negative and chaotic situations and can assist in seeing the beauty in everything and all. Jophiel can bring organization to our homes, offices, and thoughts. One can call upon Archangel Jophiel when they are feeling insecure.

Archangel Metatron–Highest of Angels

Archangel Metatron is said to watch over children in Heaven and on Earth. The archangel helps those who need focus, motivation, and organization in the starting of a new project. This archangel can help break you away from any destructive habits and align you with your soul purpose. Archangel Metatron, the angel of life, also oversees the flow of energy.

Archangel Michael–He Who Is Like God

Archangel Michael is the protector angel with his powerful sword of light. He is known to possess great strength, power, and courage. He is called upon frequently for spiritual protection and cleansing. He can release you from all fear and doubt. Archangel Michael can clear negative energies from within and around you. The archangel can protect you from negative thoughts and emotions of others toward you, you need only ask with your intent.

Archangel Raguel–Friend of God

In the book of Enoch, he is described as the overseer of all the angels. The angel ensures that all interactions between them are harmonious. He embodies unbiasedness which is why he can bring forth harmony to all relationships and situations. He can also assist with legal matters.

Archangel Raphael–He Who Heals

Archangel Raphael is known to help all creatures of God, not just humanity. The angel promotes better health, helping with both inner and outer healing. If you are feeling depressed or anxious, calling on Archangel Raphael can help to ease your worries. This archangel brings healing to those who suffer from anxiety or depression. He guides those who feel alone or lost, unmotivated or exhausted. He also guides those who heal others such as physicians, nurses, and spiritual practitioners. When taking a trip, Archangel Raphael is one you can call upon to calm any anxiety and to make sure your travel plans go smoothly.

Archangel Raziel–Secrets of God

This archangel embodies divine wisdom. In ancient Jewish lore, it is believed that Archangel Raziel hears all the universe's secrets because the archangel sits so close to the throne of God. He is also known as the angel of mysteries. If Archangel Raziel visits you, the archangel likely has some new spiritual insights or creative ideas to share with you.

Archangel Sandalphon–Highest of Angels

This archangel is said to be the twin brother of Archangel Metatron. Sandalphon means "co-brother." The archangel is known for bringing prayers to God. He is the angel of music. He rules over the music in Heaven and helps people on Earth use music to communicate with God in prayer. The archangel Sandalphon is also known to heal people from aggression.

Archangel Uriel–Light of God

The archangel's priority is to enlighten minds with new ideas, epiphanies, and insights. You can call upon Archangel Uriel to guide you in your intellectual pursuits. If you have a test to take or a business meeting to attend, this is the archangel to call upon for assistance in allowing for a smooth unfolding in those activities.

Archangel Zadkiel–Righteousness of God/Archangel of Mercy

Archangel Zadkiel is known to heal memory problems and improve other mental functions. The archangel reminds us to be grateful and encourages forgiveness. People can connect with Archangel Zadkiel to help them strengthen their connection with God/Source or "I AM Presence" and explore the concepts of mercy and forgiveness through surrendering to divine will. Once this step toward healing is made, one can move forward with healthier habits for the mind, body, and soul.

TAKEAWAYS FOR YOUR TOOLBOX

In my own experience, the divine angelic host is composed of legions upon legions of angels of pure unconditional love and light. They deliver The Creator's messages of pure unconditional love to all. And, especially in this lifetime, the Angelic Host is here to assist in the remembrance of who it is we truly are at our core essence. If they are invited with pure intention, they can be a loving, guiding light for you and can serve your highest good in many ways.

Unlike humans, the angels are not able to experience the senses as we do here on our magnificent jewel of a planet. However, they have many other qualities and abilities they can and do experience.

They are infinitely powerful beings of pure unconditional love and light. They can act at a moment's notice, if summoned by you with pure intent, and answer your call as long as it serves the highest good of all involved, aligned with divine will. It is important to mention and remember you must consciously call upon them using your pure intention, as you have free will and they will not violate free will unless asked by you to do so.

You can also make the call with your pure intent, and call upon the Sacred Fire Angels from the Great Central Sun. The Sacred Fire is the Love of God from the Great Central Sun. There is nothing more powerful in all of creation itself. Within the Sacred Fire dwells the Violet Consuming Flame and the Blue Lightning flashing, in turn, within that Violet Consuming Flame. There are legions upon legions of angels of the Sacred Fire whose soul purpose is to bring forth that Sacred Fire when you call upon it to instantaneously consume all that is less than the divine perfection of the "I AM Presence" in this world.

You can intend and ask them to ever abide with you, enfolding you in their Sacred Fire Love's Immortal, Indestructible Purity. This is a love in which no discord or human creation, that which has been created from the ego mind, can ever survive. It has the power to instantly consume and dissolve wrong and it protects all that is constructive, as well as brings forth that which is right. This is all for the fulfillment of the divine plan. This is a powerful tool and invocation you can speak daily.

The angelic host encourages us to make these calls to help not only ourselves but the human collective and the whole world as well. As you make your call and summon forth the angelic host, they are then able to instantly sweep in and bring forth that which you are asking for, as long as it is constructive, for the highest good of all, and aligned with the divine plan. When you serve the light in this way, you too are blessed beyond measure, and this is because we are all One.

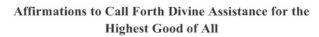

Affirmations to Call Forth Divine Assistance for the
Highest Good of All

I AM commanding, demanding, and intending, I AM the *Victory* of making the call now, and I AM consciously calling upon my own "Beloved I AM Presence" and all the Angelic Hosts, to keep me ever surrounded by the Immortal Purity of the Sacred Fire Angels that forever keeps me from all human creation, wherever I abide, move, and go, now and for all eternity itself sustained; so be it, and so it is.

I AM commanding, demanding, and intending, I AM the *Victory* that calls for the Great Angelic Host's Sacred Fire Power to Stop all human creation from ever approaching me, my loved ones, and everything and everyone under this radiation, and I find my call is fulfilled instantly now, continuously, and for all eternity itself sustained; so be it, and so it is.

I AM commanding, demanding, and intending, I AM the *Victory* of calling forth the Legions of Angels of the Sacred Fire and I AM asking them to pour their love to compel peace in my world, in, through, and all around me, wherever I abide, move, and go, now, continuously, and for all eternity itself sustained; so be it, and so it is.

I AM commanding, demanding, and intending, I AM the *Victory* of calling upon the Angelic Host's Immortal Flame of Love to come forth into outer physical action and become for me the Master of Perfection, now and for all eternity itself sustained; so be it, and so it is.

I AM commanding, demanding, and intending, I AM the *Victory* of calling for the establishment of the Angelic Host's Eternal Sacred Fire Mastery everywhere in this physical world, and everywhere in my whole world, now, continuously, and for all eternity itself sustained; so be it, and so it is.

I AM commanding, demanding, and intending, I AM the Victory of ever clothing myself in the Miracle Mantle of the Angelic Host's Heart Flame of Immortal Perfection, now and for all eternity itself sustained; so be it, and so it is.

I AM commanding, demanding, and intending, I AM the *Victory* of calling upon the Legions of Angels of the Sacred Fire to flood love to the world now and for all eternity itself sustained; so be it, and so it is.

I AM commanding, demanding, and intending, I AM the *Victory* of calling upon the Legions of Angels of the Sacred Fire to bless the whole atmosphere of Earth, and make it the comfort of the love of the Angelic Host, now and for all eternity itself sustained; so be it, and so it is.

Chapter Five

Surrendering

One day I saw an advertisement for a movie, *The Croods,* that was playing in theaters. I immediately felt an undeniable urge to go to the theater and see this animated movie, which is something I would not normally do. As much as I enjoy the movies, the urge to see something hadn't hit me in a long time.

When my son came home from school that afternoon, I was ready. "Hey, have you seen the new movie, *The Croods,* that came out? Would you like to come and see it with me?" I asked.

My thirteen-year-old scoffed, "Mom, that's a kid's movie. I think I'm too old for that."

"I know, but I have this feeling I need to see it, and I'd love it if you came along."

We went back and forth for a while, and eventually, he conceded to go to the theater with me to see the show.

Even though he'd seen ads for it, my son asked, "Mom, what's this movie about that you want to see so badly?"

I shrugged. "I don't know. I saw the ad and had a feeling that I needed to see it. I guess we'll have to find out when we get there."

As we walked in, there were hardly any people in the theater, but it wasn't completely empty. There was a mother and child seated several rows in front of us.

The Croods was set in the dinosaur age. The story revolved around a teenage girl, named Eep, who was a member of the Crood family.

Throughout the story, Eep is held at a crossroads between the desires of her family, who have a survival mindset, and a handsome young stranger, Guy, who joined their "pack" and seemingly has no fear of the world.

As I watched, I sensed the reason I was drawn to see the film. I noticed the similarities, synchronicities, and irony between my ascension journey in the physical world and Eep's journey to living a better life outside of fear. Through Eep's character growth, I was beginning to understand why the events of my own life were occurring as they were, and I could see the deeper perspective of my own situation.

About halfway through the movie, the child sitting a few rows ahead of us got out of her seat and came up to sit next to my son and me. Her mother came up to get her shortly after she sat down, but it struck me how strange it was that we'd drawn her out of her seat like that. The other mother and I laughed about it as they moved back down to their seats.

As I continued watching, I thought, *It's amazing how they captured the present conditions so well. How many people spend their whole lives living in metaphorical caves, feeling like they're safe but they aren't even really living?*

I realized many people experience life from a bubble, and until I'd begun my awakening journey, I was no exception. Often times, it seems like people are so busy living their day-to-day routines, they never allow themselves to see beyond their zone of familiarity, and more often than not, this leads to fear of the unknown and an inability to act because of that fear.

The message I was receiving from the movie was awe-inspiring. It was clearly divine, but what was more amazing to me was the fact that the message was coming through a cartoon movie, yet it was so powerful, relevant, and important.

In the movie, Eep saw a flicker of light and followed it, leading her outside of her cave. It dawned on me I was doing the same thing as I paid attention to the signs and messages coming forth into my life.

Through my own experiences, a whole new perspective was opening for me. I was being given the gift and the opportunity to follow the light, and I was doing just that. When I realized and decided it would be best for me to always be awake and conscious in each moment, I gave myself permission to welcome opportune-ities that would normally be closed off to me if I stuck with the familiar aspects of what I knew.

You never know how or when a synchronistic message could be delivered to you. If you are not fully awake and present in each *now* moment, you could miss the divine message.

The whole universe dwells within each of us and each one of us is infinite, divine intelligence. Therefore, we are not being "taught" anything. We are *remembering* All That Is, who we are one with, and who has always been within us. When we allow ourselves to live in the moment, we become aware of all the synchronistic messages flowing to us from The Divine. We are able to stay on our path, serving our soul's purpose, which is always serving *our* highest good and the highest good of all, simultaneously.

Love's messages are pure and blissful,
And give you clear sight.
So, you may discern for yourself,
What is the light.

Love is truthful,
And love is honest as can be.
It exposes all,
With its luminosity.

So, listen to your own heart,
For it will always tell you true…
If it doesn't have the qualities above,
It may not be for you.

For love always uplifts,
And cheers you on.
Love only gives compliments,
So, may all else be gone.

Love will always find the blessing,
In absolutely everything.
It only brings happy thoughts,
That make your heart sing.

For it is who you are,
And have always been.
You will recognize it easily,
For it dwells within.

It was toward the end of the movie the message I was meant to receive became very clear. When it got to the climax of the story and the big decisions were being made for their family, the Croods were left standing in an unknown space of almost being forced to trust. The world they knew was crumbling around them and it was time to leave the perceived safety of the cave, the world they knew, for the real safety of the solid ground beyond. They couldn't see the other side of the valley, but Eep was willing to lead the way and guide her family to a better life.

As I watched, I received another urge to glance away from the screen to my right. As I turned, I noticed Archangel Michael, clear as day, standing about six feet away from me. I could barely believe my eyes. He stood approximately eleven feet tall, and he looked like a true warrior. He wasn't looking at me, he was looking intently at the movie screen, so I turned my attention back to the movie as well.

The message coming from the movie was clear. As the family put their faith in each other and leaped into the unknown of a brand-new world, I too was meant to surrender myself to the unknown and follow the light, even if I didn't fully understand it or I couldn't see the path ahead clearly. The Divine would always be there to catch me and would never lead me astray.

As The Divine asked me to trust and to follow the light, so are we all being asked to trust and follow the light. In each moment, we are being given the gift to see the divinity and the highest light within ourselves and within all others. We are asked to do this no matter what outer appearances seem to be. In truth, we are all infinite love and light at our core. It is all about seeing through what appears to be on the surface and looking deeper and gaining a higher perspective to see the truth.

When you allow yourself to see only light within all, something truly magical happens for you and for others. Not only does your life become divinely blessed with all you desire or better but seeing only light also allows for others to see it within themselves. It is all an inside job. It all starts with you.

The external world is merely a mirror to your feelings and beliefs about self at any given moment. It all begins with loving yourself and knowing you are worthy of love. The entire universe dwells within you, and you are one with it. Therefore, as you love yourself, you are loving all of creation itself simultaneously. As you place your hand on your own heart and say, "I love you," to yourself, you are then telling all of creation itself you love it too.

You are worthy of all good and magnificent things as the divine creator you are, and it is now time to own that knowing.

One of the things necessary on your spiritual path is your own ability to fully trust The Divine.

For me, surrendering was, and is, a gradual, continuous process. I knew, through previous experience, everything would work out exactly as it needed to, as all is in divine time and order. However, there were certain aspects I couldn't see and did not understand the benefits of at the time of their happening. Nonetheless, I knew deep down through my surrendering to The Divine everything would most certainly work out for my highest good. I trusted The Divine and moved forward.

You and your divine purpose,
Are one and the same.
It's already within you,
There's nothing to gain.

There is only an allowance,
For what is to be…
For it has already been created,
All by me.

It all exists right here,
And right now.
So, no need for striving,
Or needing to know how.

Just a simple surrender,
Will do just fine.
And a leaving of that,
Which does not serve behind.

A shedding of all old programming,
Ways of being, and old beliefs too…
Yes, we will leave all behind,
That does not serve you.

I will polish you then,
Until you sparkle and shine…
Showing you ever so clearly,
What has been the whole time.

For deep within,
What I have been wanting you to see…
When you peel off all the layers,
That which remains is me.

I AM That I AM.

My sessions with Divine Archangel Raphael continued. I was able to ask anything during these channeled sessions and it was a tremendous help to me.

Of course, your "I AM Presence" is always your Source for everything and all. As I knew free will was always at play, I received divine help when I intended and asked for it. Because I was still experiencing lingering medical issues, I started asking for help from my "I AM Presence," The Divine, in that arena.

One day, I decided to vacuum and clean up a bit. I had the television on a music station. It was playing spiritual music that was uplifting, and I listened to it often when I cleaned my apartment. I had the volume loud to be able to hear the music over the vacuum cleaner. I was in the process of vacuuming the living room when a song began to play. I had never heard this song before, but I really liked the tune, and it was upbeat.

It was by the band The Newsboys. As I vacuumed and listened to the lyrics, doing my best to sing along, I heard a lyric in the song that stopped me dead in my tracks. I quickly turned off the vacuum and stood there staring at the television. I don't think I moved for several minutes. I focused my attention on each word of the song as it played.

I knew it was my "I AM Presence," God, speaking directly to me, and it was a message of the utmost importance. The title of the song was "Save Your Life." I don't know how to explain it, but I knew intuitively I needed to pay close attention to this divine message.

The Divine, through the lyrics of the song, was asking me to surrender to divine will, letting me know this would most certainly be for my highest good. I also felt The Divine was communicating to me this message was very important and to pay close attention to it because my actual life depended on it. I knew, at the time, that this was my choice point. I knew what I did next would determine if I lived or transitioned. There was only one choice for me... *I was all in!*

It was never a question for me. I chose to live that day, aligning myself with my highest timeline. I chose love and continue to do so.

As my transcendental experiences continued, I came to understand we are here for important reasons. I could feel the love The Creative Source had for me. I was determined more than ever to evolve and expand and to open my heart even further. I had absolutely no idea where I was going but I was surrendering to divine will, and I was asking and intending for my "I AM Presence" to lead the way... and so it was.

TAKEAWAYS FOR YOUR TOOLBOX

One of the most powerful archangels of all, Archangel Michael, was asking me to trust and have faith in the highest aspect of who it is I AM. At the time, I felt this was a direct communication from The Divine letting me know it had my back. I was to relinquish all control to The Divine, with full trust, allowing the universe to lead me on my path of least resistance for my highest good.

This is being asked of all of us right now. We are not meant to know the *how* of it, we are meant to trust, to go with the flow, and surrender to The Divine, our own "Beloved I AM Presence," who has all of that handled for us on our behalf.

Surrendering to infinite divine wisdom solves any possible issues you may have faster than if you try to handle them yourself. You are never meant to do anything alone. You are meant to hand over, through surrendering to The Divine, all your perceived problems. You are meant to hand it literally over to your own "Mighty I AM Presence," who is the only invincible solver of any problem ever, in all of creation and existence. All perceived problems are but to compel a recognition of God, the "Mighty I AM Presence," as the supreme controller and activity in all things.

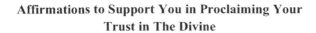

Affirmations to Support You in Proclaiming Your Trust in The Divine

I AM commanding, demanding, and intending, I AM the *Victory* of being one with divine flow as I am continuously choosing to go with the flow of my infinitely abundant, benevolent, unconditionally loving universe who loves me unconditionally beyond measure now and for all eternity sustained; so be it, and so it is.

I AM commanding, demanding, and intending, I AM the *Victory* of relinquishing all control, urgency, expectations, and judgments to The Divine for my highest good and for the highest good of all I am one with now and for all eternity sustained; so be it, and so it is.

I AM commanding, demanding, and intending, I AM the *Victory* of choosing to ever evolve and expand through miracle consciousness, synchronicity, pure divine flow, pure unconditional love, and gratitude; so be it, and so it is.

I AM commanding, demanding, and intending, I have full faith, trust, and belief in the divine process and the divine plan which I AM ever one with, now and for all eternity itself sustained; so be it, and so it is.

I AM commanding, demanding, and intending that I AM the *Victory* of surrendering now to divine will, my own "Beloved, Mighty I AM Presence," the highest, divine aspect of who it is that I AM; so be it, and so it is.

I AM commanding, demanding, and intending that I AM the *Victory* of surrendering now all of the energies that are less than the divine perfection of my own "Mighty I AM Presence," the highest, divine aspect of who it is that I AM, letting them all go now and I am releasing them to my "I AM Presence" to be instantly dissolved and consumed in the light of my "I AM That I AM That I AM Presence"; so be it, and so it is.

Chapter Six
Energy

*H*aving received The Divine's message from Archangel Michael during the movie *The Croods* to take a leap of faith and having been told by Archangel Raphael, in the angel's words, that I was a spontaneous, direct healer, I decided to sign up for some healing classes.

I had read about several different types of healing modalities and one of those modalities, Integrated Energy Therapy (IET), fascinated me the most.

Integrated Energy Therapy sessions work directly with your body's cellular memory and energy field to get the *issues out of your tissues* for good. The sessions include using angelic energy to gently release limiting energy patterns from your past. The sessions empower you, balance your life in the present, and allow for you to embody your full potential as you move into your future.

Since I already had a strong connection with the divine angelic realm, working as I was with Divine Archangel Raphael and Archangel Michael, I decided to sign up to be a certified IET practitioner.

IET specifically works with the energy of the nine divine angels, Ariel, Raphael, Gabriel, Celestina, Faith, Cassiel, Daniel, Sarah, and Michael, and I was more than excited.

During my search for healing modalities, I came across a woman who offered Integrated Energy Sessions. I made a call to the instructor, and I set up an appointment to begin. I was eager to start; however, the IET courses, levels one, two, and three, cost several hundred dollars. I knew that I would have added funds in my account that upcoming Monday, the day my class was to start which was concerning to me.

I wouldn't be able to go to the bank, withdraw the funds, and arrive on time for my first IET class. I was not even sure if the funds would be in my account that early on Monday morning. I didn't know what to do to solve this dilemma, but I knew the class was important.

It was the Saturday before my first IET class, and I was sitting on the sidelines of my son's baseball game. Halfway through the game, I glanced down at my phone, having the inclination to check my bank account balance. I opened my banking app and logged into my account, and I could not believe my eyes. All my *pendente lite* funds had arrived two days early, and on a weekend no less.

This was odd and had never happened to me before. My funds were always deposited into my account on a scheduled day of the month.

As soon as I saw my bank account balance, I knew The Divine had blessed me, and they had intervened and intentionally placed those funds in my account early. I said a prayer immediately and thanked and expressed my gratitude to my Divine Source for this amazing gift.

When you are in alignment with your "I AM Presence," you cannot help but receive all that your heart desires. Being one with your "I AM Presence" is being aligned with divine will. As you are aligned with divine will, you are loving self and all as self; you are also knowing there is truly nothing and no one to forgive, as all is always divine perfection. You are at a level of conscious awareness and knowing that all is always in perfect divine time and order, so how could there ever be a mistake? There can't be. Choosing to live your life attuned with the vibration and frequency of gratitude, and the knowing that you are worthy of receiving all the infinite divine blessings and gifts that your "I AM Presence" has to bestow upon you will surely bring forth those blessings into your experience.

"All things are possible,"
Are the words of the day.
The Creative Source of All That Is,
Can always make a way.

There are infinite solutions,
That your eyes may not see.
There is always a way,
When you think a way can't be.

For out of the ethers,
The answer appears,
So, no need for upset,
Crying or tears.

Just knock on the door and ask...
And it will be given to you.
The door will fly open,
And your miracle will shine through.

All is well.

It became a regular occurrence for me to see white, sparkling twinkles lighting up my carpet as well as in the air itself. I came to know and understand this was The Divine's way of letting me know I was always safe and protected. They were letting me know they were present with me, and all was well.

I was going through a major energetic cleansing process, and even though I had to go through it by myself, The Divine was holding my hand through it all.

There were days upon days of clearing out and releasing old belief systems, old ways of being, old programming, and all that did not serve me. I would sometimes spend several hours a day, in a seated position, intending and calling forth The Divine to assist me in clearing density and energetic debris I had accumulated over lifetimes.

It was not a pleasant process; however, it was a beneficial one for me, and I am grateful to The Divine for it. The energy I was clearing, at times, felt like giant, energetic bubbles I was releasing. It would release out of my field, through my crown (the top of my head), back to the universal grid, back to the light. It was exhausting.

There were times when I did not think I would survive it. However, I was so blessed, and still am today, to have Divine Archangel Raphael in my life as a guide. I was grateful to be going through these processes of my ascension divinely guided.

One day I invited a friend over to my apartment. I met her at Soulutions, and we became fast friends. She, too, was interested in spirituality, and she asked if I could give her an oracle card reading.

Oracle cards, for those who aren't familiar with them, are similar to a deck of playing cards. They have two sides and are usually adorned with beautiful artwork. They also have messages written on them. As you choose a card for yourself or for another because the Law of Attraction is always at play in the universe, the cards you pick indicate and give you a reading of what you are offering up vibrationally. Therefore, they are always an accurate reading of the energy you are radiating at any given moment.

My friend had some questions regarding a love interest of hers.

We sat down in my living room, and I let her pick out the deck she wanted to use for her reading. I could feel my friend was hoping to get a message that her love interest would reciprocate with similar feelings of love.

During our session, all the messages from the oracle cards she chose were telling her to move on from the relationship in question.

During the reading, there were many sparkles of white light flashing sporadically all around us in the living room. It was my feeling that The Divine, along with the vehicle of the oracle card reading, were doing their best to deliver an important message for my friend's highest good.

Unfortunately, she was not understanding or hearing the message. She asked me to shuffle again and give her a second reading. I believe she thought the cards might turn out differently.

I knew this was not going to be the case, but I shuffled the oracle cards and displayed them once again for her to select from. Once again, my friend picked the same cards. She started to laugh nervously.

I explained, "You can never pick an incorrect card in your reading. Everything you put out to the universe is being mirrored back to you and the cards are reflecting that. The answers are here whether you decide to listen to them or not."

She asked, "Can't we do it one more time?"

I said, "The Law of Attraction is always at play in the universe. The cards you pick are for you in this situation, and they are accurate based on your energy in this moment, your point of attraction."

I could see she still was holding onto her wishes regarding her love interest and was yet to be "on board" with what The Divine was communicating to her.

I gathered the oracle cards up once more and placed them all in the upright position before I shuffled them once again. Just as I was about to shuffle the deck, I glanced down at the oracle cards. Every other card had been turned upside down throughout the entire deck. I could not believe it. At that point, my friend had no choice but to finally concede and hear the message that was profoundly being delivered to her. By flipping the cards before the shuffle, The Divine was sending another clear message that the answer was already in her hands.

My friend finally came to the realization the relationship in question was not serving her highest good, and she decided she was going to end it before it even started. In this instance, The Divine resorted to placing something she couldn't deny in her path, allowing her to receive the message intended for her highest good.

This was another reminder for me to pay attention. The universe is always delivering messages to us. The important question becomes, "Are we allowing ourselves to be in the receptive mode, allowing ourselves to listen and receive the messages continuously being delivered?"

In Soulutions, I would watch people give themselves oracle card readings. They would choose cards they did not feel were for them. I then watched as they placed them back in the deck, reshuffled and dealt them again, in hopes of picking something different. I used to do the same exact thing when I first started on my journey.

I did not understand then that all is always in perfect divine time and order. I did not understand when I surrendered and aligned myself with divine will, and intended my "I AM Presence" to work through me, on my behalf, picking all my cards for me, through absolute, pure, unconditional love. I was always going to pick the card for me even if I shuffled the deck fifty times.

It did not matter how I pulled the card out of the deck; I was going to pick the one I was a vibrational match to, the one that was always meant for me. There is no picking a wrong card in an oracle card reading, like there are no coincidences in life. All is in perfect divine time and order, and everything is always serving your highest good. All is always divine perfection.

Oracle cards can often be beautiful works of art. They were such a fun activity for me. I enjoyed not knowing what card I would pull, coupled with the excitement of knowing my card would always be perfect for me due to the natural laws of the universe. However, as my consciousness evolved, I came to understand and know that using oracle cards is still seeking for information outside of oneself.

All of us are now being strongly encouraged, by The Divine, for our own highest good, to always turn inward for any answer we may be seeking. Your own "Beloved I AM Presence" always has any answer to any question you could possibly have. It also is the only true solver of any perceived problem you could possibly ever have. Like anything else, it takes practice in remembering to continuously turn inward, because all the answers you seek lie within you always.

Sometimes reminders are needed,
To remember what to hold dear.
Sometimes reminders are needed,
To choose love not fear.

Sometimes reminders are needed,
And placed right in front of you…
Allowing you to go nowhere,
Until the love you are shines through.

Sometimes reminders are needed,
To show you how creative you are,
Allowing you to dream in ways,
You haven't done thus far.

Sometimes reminders are needed,
To see you truly are blessed…
That you are absolute, sheer divine perfection,
And nothing that is less.

I went through many healing initiations during this time spent with my friend Simona. She, along with my "I AM Presence" helped me to remember the essence of who it is I truly am.

During our time together, Simona began to channel more divine beings of infinite love and light. I had several conversations with Jesus and many other Ascended Light Beings who were channeled through her.

I was also practicing my own channeling abilities during my sessions with Simona. It was all so new to me, and it was comforting; I found it helpful to have a friend who was already channeling.

One Christmas and New Year's Eve I had to miss completely. When I say miss completely, I mean I was not able to take part in my traditional holiday festivities with my family.

During one of my sessions with Simona, right before the Christmas holiday, she was asked by The Divine to help facilitate a healing for me. This was not an ordinary healing, as I quickly discovered. It was a process where I was given, in a way, new life and new energy. My energies were first completely cleared, and then I was wrapped in what I can only describe as etheric gauze.

Immediately after that process, I was super sensitive to almost all energies. I needed to be alone for almost three months. The only people who could be near me, and who I felt comfortable around my energetic body were Simona and my son. My son had to explain to my family members as to why I could not attend that year's holiday gatherings.

Energetically, I was raw and extremely vulnerable. I needed time to build my energy body back to its strength and fortification. My family lived right around the corner from me and I was not able to see or talk to them for the entire holiday season. If I did, I would start to feel their energy and it was not a pleasant experience for me.

During that time, my son asked me to call a department store to order a gift for him so he could give it to his grandmother on Christmas morning. A salesperson from the department store answered the phone, and my whole body started to energetically move in what felt like waves. I had to hang up the phone immediately and lie down. I realized I could not even make a single phone call without feeling an unpleasant sensation energetically in my field.

Believe it or not, my son completely understood what I was going through. He went to his grandparents' home for Christmas and did his best to explain my situation. He has always had an intuitive knowledge about things and was in full understanding of what was taking place.

With my immediate family, on the other hand, and rightly so, it was a different story.

During the time spent in monthly sessions with Simona, I went through profound shifts, and I had to leave certain people and situations in my life.

At first, this was a bit difficult. However, as time went on and I experienced it more, I came to understand it is the way of it. As we each expand our consciousness, we outgrow certain things, situations, and even certain people. Things that used to work and serve you for your highest good do not any longer and you need to move on. This does not mean you must avoid those certain people and situations forever. Hopefully, as time passes, you will be more equipped to navigate and direct the energy as you will be more in control of it, and you will remember you are a master of it. This will be because you will have gained a higher perspective and gathered many tools to help as a result of doing your own inner work.

When people or places or situations move out of our lives, it is never personal, and it is never anyone's fault. There is never any blame whatsoever. It is the universe's way of saying to you it is time to move on to a new experience and these experiences are always serving your highest good and the highest good of all simultaneously. You can stay in alignment with your soul's purpose by allowing yourself to always follow your joy.

Your feelings about things, situations, and people is the way your "I AM Presence" steers and guides you, at any given moment, toward what brings you the most happiness and inner peace.

Calling you deeper now,
Within the flow.
Your heart, as you trust more,
And hence you go.

Deeper and deeper,
And deeper ever still.
In the cavern of light,
Of faith, of divine will.

It's an ocean so deep,
No bottom is there to be.
For this is infiniteness,
An always expanding luminosity.

So, focus now, on that which is only love,
And on that which is only light,
And your journey ever changing,
Will be one of pure delight.

TAKEAWAYS FOR YOUR TOOLBOX

You are a pure spirit having a physical experience. All of creation and existence is energy, love energy. There is nothing else. This is who you are as well. Energy is neither created nor destroyed, it simply changes form; therefore, you are an eternal being of infinite love and light, continuously changing form and ever evolving and expanding to higher light. You are vast, limitless, boundless eternal love and light. You are so much more than your physical body. You are one with all things, as all things are one with you.

Everything in all of creation and existence has already been created. I will repeat that because I feel this is important, and it was a very important nugget of truth for me to grasp in being a successful conscious co-creator of my own reality. *Everything in all of creation and existence has already been created.* Everything exists right *now*. There is no *time*. Time is an illusion we as a human collective agreed to create to experience this Earth realm. Since you are literally all of creation and all of existence, everything lies within you now. If you can think of something with your thoughts, it exists for you to experience. You would not even be able to think of it if it did not already exist.

The Great Ascended Masters of Light continue to remind us, for our own benefit, to watch and pay close attention to what we are focusing on. They are reminding us of this because that which you focus on is like a request or an order placed to the universe. It informs the universe you would like more of that thing you are placing your attention on. This is how the universe operates. Also, the universe only has one and only one answer for you, and that answer is always an emphatic *Yes*. It's similar to the universe saying to you, "I will give to you what you are thinking and feeling and believing and placing your attention on at all times without fail." You can see now why having a harmonious thinking mind and feeling world is beneficial to you.

All of this is great news. If everything is love energy, and love energy is all of creation and existence, and you are one with that which you most definitely are whether conscious of it or not, then it literally becomes a picking and choosing of that which you wish to experience. You are the creator of your own reality. And, when you truly own this knowing and operate from this space, then you begin to allow yourself to choose that which you wish to experience. You achieve this through the direction of your own thoughts, and that which you are focusing on and intending for self. When you can maintain harmony in your thinking mind and feeling world you have reached mastery. You become a master of energy, able to direct your thoughts and bring forth spontaneously that which you wish and desire to experience.

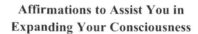

**Affirmations to Assist You in
Expanding Your Consciousness**

I AM commanding, demanding, and intending, I AM the *Victory* of the oneness and the consciousness and the pure knowing I AM my soul as form; so be it, and so it is.

I AM commanding, demanding, and intending, I AM the *Victory* of ever being filled with vitality, strength, and positive life-force energy, now and continuously and for all eternity itself sustained; so be it, and so it is.

I AM commanding, demanding, and intending, I AM the *Victory* of always being at peace, relaxed, and in perfect divine harmony and balance in all areas of my life, reality, and experience, now and continuously and for all eternity itself sustained; so be it, and so it is.

I AM commanding, demanding, and intending, I AM the *Victory* of the oneness, the consciousness, and the pure knowing that I AM a clear, sentient being of light, now and for all eternity itself sustained; so be it, and so it is.

I AM commanding, demanding, and intending my inner world is filled with positivity and it reflects my outer world. I bring calm, positivity, and harmony wherever I abide, move, and go, now and for all eternity itself sustained; so be it, and so it is.

I AM commanding, demanding, and intending, I AM the *Victory* of the oneness and the consciousness and the pure knowing that what fulfills me, energizes me, and brings me pure joy, is what is manifesting in my life right now; so be it, and so it is.

Chapter Seven

Healing

*D*uring my early twenties into my late thirties, I suffered from a chronic arthritis-related condition afflicting me to the point of needing daily medication. It was getting to a point where, even with the medication, I was experiencing daily low-grade fevers, and I was meeting my doctor monthly while we were trying to sort out new treatment options. At the same time, we were also trying to wean me off all my long-term medications as my doctor wanted to see if he could find a minimum level that could also keep my symptoms at bay. We both wanted to see me taking the least number of medications possible.

While going through this, I was also experiencing deep, personal transformation as I leaned into and put my full faith and trust in The Divine. Great shifts were happening in my life, and I was taking notice of them.

One day, I went to a gynecologist for a routine exam. Once the exam was concluded, I could tell the physician's assistant looked concerned. She didn't provide me with any details, but she did ask me if I would come back in a few weeks for a follow-up appointment.

It was the beginning of spring, and it was tradition for my son and me to travel to Clearwater Beach to watch the spring training for the Philadelphia Phillies. I was also still going through my divorce proceedings, so when March arrived, I started feeling some anxiety about not having the funds for us to go.

My son asked, "Mom, have you made the reservations yet?"

My anxiety levels rose at the mention of possibly not being able to go on our trip and letting my son down. I pondered asking him if I could borrow the money from him since he had quite the savings from receiving gifts over his birthdays and holidays, but I decided against it. Even though I knew I'd be able to pay him back after the divorce settled, which was months away, I didn't want to take anything from him for the sake of a trip we didn't *need* to go on.

I pondered what to do next. As it got closer to the time we'd need to leave if we were going to go, I resigned myself to telling him we weren't going to make it this year.

I decided to sleep on it for one more night before I broke the news to my son. I knew he'd be disappointed, but there wasn't anything I could do in our current circumstances.

After having fallen asleep, during my sleep time, a huge *whoosh* of energy overcame me. My whole space was full of brilliant blue light energy. It was like a power surge in the air I could feel in my whole being. Then, my perception of time shifted, and everything was moving in slow motion.

I was aware I was in a dream. In fact, there was no way what I was experiencing was *not* a dream, but it was possibly the most lucid dream I've ever experienced to date.

After the energy surge, I was wide awake in my awareness. I remember giggling and saying to myself, "Wow, this isn't my energy," as the blue energy continued to be present, lingering. Even though this energy felt new to me, it managed to put me at ease.

I sat upright in bed, turned my head and I instinctually glanced toward the left corner of my room. There I saw a man standing in the corner staring intently at me with a kind, focused expression.

I gasped when I noticed him, and at that moment a name floated clearly into my awareness, *Jesus.*

While he didn't say his name out loud, I knew his telepathic communication was simply him introducing himself to me, but I also knew who he was before he told me. He continued to repeat his name to me telepathically, and he moved away from the corner of the room and nearer to my bed. The telepathic communication was like a balm to ease me into simply being for this shared moment.

We locked eyes as he walked over to me, and there was a deep familiarity there. I recognized him and knew him from more than this brief dream interaction—like a being from a former life. I imagine he appeared to me that way to give me more comfort and ease in his presence.

With a focused look, he stood on the left side of the bed and placed his hand on my higher heart. He gently pushed me down, so I was lying flat again before he walked to the end of my bed, knelt, and proceeded to place his hands inside of me. It was about thirty seconds before he seemingly healed me and then pulled his hand away. All the while, he continued to project his name into my mind to keep me calm and help me feel safe.

The lucid dream shifted and again I found myself with Jesus, walking through a mall food court. He was walking slightly behind me as we approached an ice cream vendor, and we both placed an order for ice cream.

When Jesus placed his order, the woman taking our orders said, "I'm sorry, we don't have that flavor."

A man who was out of my eyesight yelled out from the back, "You don't know what you're talking about, we definitely have that flavor."

They bickered for a moment before they handed us our ice cream. I giggled at the ridiculousness of it all before I reached down to grab my wallet from my purse and realized I didn't have my purse at all. It should have been slung over my shoulder and it wasn't.

I started panicking, wondering how I was going to pay for this ice cream we'd already started eating before Jesus motioned for me to look at him.

Over his left shoulder, he was carrying a brown satchel. He opened it and inside I saw my son's rainbow-colored, surfer-styled, cloth wallet. It was an unmistakable design, and I knew right away it was my son's.

Jesus pulled the wallet out and handed it to me, asking me, without words, to use my son's money to pay for our ice cream.

Once again, the scenery of my lucid dream changed, and Jesus and I were standing in a neighborhood of brownstone houses. I recognized it as my aunt and uncle's neighborhood, and we were indeed standing outside of their house. I had a clear view into one of the windows from the sidewalk, and it appeared to me my aunt was lying on what looked like a massage table.

As I observed more, I could tell something was wrong with my aunt as my uncle was frantic and seemed to be panicking. He was trying to help my aunt, but nothing seemed to be working.

I glanced at the front door and saw Jesus waiting there with his hand on the doorknob. He looked directly at me with urgency, and without saying a word he indicated I needed to come over and open the front door for him.

I wondered, *Why can't you open it, Jesus? You're standing right there.* But for some reason, it was significant that I opened the door.

When I turned the knob, the door swung open with ease, and I was suddenly at my aunt's side. Jesus stood near my aunt's heart area, and I was near her abdomen. My uncle wasn't in my direct sight anymore, but I could hear him clearly. He was extremely distressed and continuously yelling for help.

It appeared my aunt had stopped breathing.

Jesus laid his hand on my aunt's throat, and she took a gasp of air and sat upright. My uncle became hysterical with joy and started shouting gratitude at the neighbor for saving his wife's life.

Both Jesus and I were invisible to everyone else in the room.

I watched the celebration of my uncle before I turned to speak to Jesus and noticed he already had his back to me and was walking away. It seemed his work was done, and he was leaving.

Jesus walked right through the side of my aunt's home and then disappeared in an instant. I immediately woke up from my lucid dream and found myself sitting upright in my bed.

The quiet elegance of stillness,
So very pure.
Always so enticing,
In its perfect divine allure.

Timeless, boundless, infinite,
And eternal too…
There's nothing in this space,
That cannot be through you.

For now has no care,
Of what's come before.
And it seeks not,
To look beyond any door.

Now is now is now,
And forever will be.
Now is ease and grace,
In all its simplicity.

You are here now,
And now you are.
There is no such thing,
As near or far.

Nowhere to travel,
And nothing to achieve.
It's all now within you,
If you just believe.

I received powerful messages and healing from The Divine through my lucid dream with Jesus that night. With my aunt and uncle, I felt I was reminded that anyone could have come to save my aunt's life, even a neighbor, but they would be working in co-creation with The Divine Source to heal and save the life. I realized even though many could not see them, there were always divine, benevolent forces of light working and serving the highest good of all when we ask and intend them to do so.

I also know when Jesus put his hands inside of my body, he was instantaneously healing me, seeing me in my truth as whole and complete. When I awoke from my lucid dream with Jesus, I immediately felt a cramping in my abdominal area. The cramping continued for a couple weeks before it subsided. This was even further validation, although I did not need it, that something had miraculously occurred within me—my spontaneous healing.

When I went to my follow-up appointment at my doctor's office and the physician's assistant checked me over again, whatever she had seen the first time was gone.

She said, "Well, I saw something here I really didn't like the look of. I brought you back because I wanted to be sure of my findings before I made a diagnosis and told you about it, but it seems to have disappeared, and I've never seen something like that happen."

I wasn't sure whether to share the experiences I had with Jesus with my physician's assistant; however, I thought, *What the heck.* This is my truth and it really happened.

I decided I was not going to hold back my truth for anything. There is a profound reason why this was occurring for me, and it needed to be shared to assist others.

I spoke my full truth to her. I explained the profound experience I had gone through, and I explained I knew in my heart my healing had been facilitated by Jesus and it had occurred during my lucid dream.

She seemed to agree after having listened to what I had to say.

She kept saying, "I've never seen this condition heal itself in anyone before now."

It truly felt good to share my experience with her at that moment.

Absolutely all things are possible through and with The Divine, and there are never any exceptions to this truth.

The other divine gift from my dream was the divine communicating to me that it was more than okay for me to go ahead and use my son's funds for our trip to Florida. By seeing my son's wallet in the dream, and using his money to pay for ice cream, I was being presented with the wisdom that my son would be gracious and accept the fact I would be giving the money back soon enough.

I felt the final revelation and divine gift bestowed upon me during this lucid dream is I could, as Jesus did, see the wholeness within myself and within all. This allowed for my own healing to occur which was facilitated by Jesus.

I was taken by Jesus to my aunt's side in that lucid dream to show me that truth. We are all powerful creators. We are all extensions of Source Energy, the Master Creator. We each, if we allow and intend for it to be so, can direct the power that creates worlds, which is continuously flowing through each of us at any given moment.

As we continuously allow ourselves to see the light, the wholeness, the completeness, and the divine perfection within all things, we allow for those things to return to the wholeness they have always been. When you hold that core truth in your heart, that all is love and all is light no matter what, something appears in the external world, and miracles can unfold.

During my lucid dream, in the moment I was healed, and in the moment my aunt was healed, Jesus had seen the divine perfection within both of us. This allowed for my aunt and me to see, on a deeper level, our own divine perfection. It then enabled both my aunt and me to rebalance and to align ourselves to the divine perfection we each are and have always been.

In the presence of one who already knows and sees our divine perfection, a spontaneous healing was able to manifest. In Jesus's presence, in his pure knowing of who he truly is, and in his pure knowing of what and who all else is, all beings and things can rebalance and recalibrate themselves back to the wholeness they are in truth.

We each have this same power within us. It all begins with knowing who it is you are and who it is everyone and everything else is, which is pure love. We are all Source Energy. We are all one, and we are all whole and complete as we are in each now moment.

It then becomes a remembering of that truth in each and every moment. When you come to truly know you are already whole and complete as you are, it must be so. The universal law states you cannot help but receive that which you know you are one with.

My son and I ended up having a lovely trip to Clearwater Beach, Florida that year.

Off-
To my favorite place I go,
To envision a world,
I've come to know.

One of perfect health, happiness,
And all dreams come true.
For this is already present,
Within the Creator's heart, within you.

There is only perfection,
Now, continuously, and forevermore,
For this is the promise,
So steadfast and sure.

Place all attention on well-being,
And only light,
For this is all that flows to you,
This magical night.

And as you remember this promise,
This truth deep within,
A calming, gentle whisper,
Is allowed to begin.

It says so crisply,
And ever so clear...
"Remember who you are, beloved,
And have no fear."

For you are creating this,
All as you go...
And as you focus on only love,
Only love, you will come to know.

All is well.

TAKEAWAYS FOR YOUR TOOLBOX

This miraculous visit from the Master of Love was to remind me all things are possible through and with divine love. It was also a reminder that we are all healthy, whole, and complete just as we are.

We are all one with our Creator, who is divine perfection always. Therefore, we are also divine perfection. When we begin to love ourselves, prioritizing our joy, first and foremost, and when we begin to love all others as ourselves, and when we accept life as it is showing up for us and love it too, miracles begin to unfold. We are then able to see the divine perfection we have always been, and that perfection is then mirrored back to us in our entire experience of life.

Sometimes the things we need to do in order to heal can be uncomfortable, but we can always choose to navigate through them with help from The Divine.

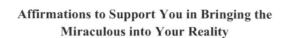

Affirmations to Support You in Bringing the Miraculous into Your Reality

I AM commanding, demanding, and intending, I AM the *Victory* of choosing to be one with the pure knowing all things are possible through and with The Divine now and always; so be it, and so it is.

I AM commanding, demanding, and intending, I AM the *Victory* of choosing that I AM always one with the pure knowing I can be, do, and have anything, now and always; so be it, and so it is.

I AM commanding, demanding, and intending, I AM the *Victory* of choosing I AM always one with the divine miraculous, and divine miracles are happening all around me. I AM always the *Victory* of expecting the divine miraculous in my life, all now, continuously, and for all eternity itself sustained; so be it, and so it is.

I AM commanding, demanding, and intending, I AM the *Victory* of choosing to always be one with the pure knowing I AM always healthy, whole, and complete as I AM; so be it, and so it is.

I AM commanding, demanding, and intending, I AM the *Victory* of choosing to only see the divinity and the highest light within myself and within All That Is, I AM, that dwells within me at any given moment, now, continuously, and for all eternity itself sustained; so be it, and so it is.

I AM commanding, demanding, and intending, I AM the *Victory* of the oneness and the consciousness and the pure knowing that everything is always a divine blessing and gift for me, at any given moment, now, continuously, and for all eternity itself sustained; so be it, and so it is.

I AM commanding, demanding, and intending, I AM the *Victory* of the pure knowing I AM worthy because "I AM That I AM" and in that infinite, divine worthiness, I AM ready to receive all of the infinite divine blessings and gifts my divine, benevolent "Mighty I AM Presence" has to bestow upon me and bless me with now and for all eternity itself sustained; so be it, and so it is.

Chapter Eight

Asking

*O*nce I dove into and made a commitment to do my inner work, things really started to open up for me. I found myself spending several hours a day clearing my energy field. I'd do my best to give myself breaks; however, I felt a constant need to clear density and energetic debris so it wouldn't accumulate.

When I cleared my energy field, I always had the assistance of The Divine to guide and aid me. It was relieving because I found it more and more difficult to keep up, the deeper I went into my clearing practice. It was even getting to the point that if I waited too long (from an energetic standpoint), I would find it difficult to move and even breathe.

I rarely ventured outside of my home during this period of energy work. I was getting into the work of clearing out lifetimes of density and discordant energy in my energy field.

Of course, I knew the awareness and feeling of it was a blessing. It let me know there was still work to be done, but I was getting into the densest energy, which meant I was getting down to the bottom of the proverbial barrel. However, I longed for and needed a reprieve.

The Divine was fully aware of this and came quickly to my aid with my asking.

One evening, when I was sitting watching television, I felt lightheaded. I wasn't sure what it was, so I immediately, instinctually shook it off. As soon as I shook my head, the dizziness went away for a little while. After about half an hour or so, the foggy, lightheaded feeling, and the dizziness returned.

I felt like something heavy was trying to make its way into my being through my crown chakra at the top of my head. I shook it off again, but I was also tired enough I decided to go lie down in my bed and try to sleep.

When I was starting to drift off, the sensation of whatever was trying to gain access to my energy field returned at the top of my head once again. This time, I was far too tired to shake off whatever energy this was, and it was too determined to have its way with me to fight it any longer. I drifted off and the next thing I remember was sensing intuitively this tiny light being hovering over my body.

Please turn to me for everything,
Just place it all in my hand.
For nothing is too small for me,
And nothing is too grand.

I AM the only invincible solver,
Of any problem,
Please know this to be true.
And when you let go,

And surrender it to me,
I will take it from you.
Absorbed it will then be,
Back into the All.

For this burden alone,
Was not yours to carry,
No most certainly,
Not at all.

We are a team you and I,
The absolute very best.
Your job is to solely hand it over,
And allow me to do the rest.

So, let's begin this partnership now,
As it was always meant to be.
Surrender all your troubles and woes,
And I will set you free.

While I'd experienced light beings before, this sensation was new to me. I reached up out of curiosity to feel the entity hovering over me, and I felt this tiny head directly above my head.

As soon as I felt the head, I lowered my hands and cringed a bit, not meaning to be offending a being who was clearly of the light and had come to help me.

The being didn't seem to mind though; it had its own mission and it started pulling at something on the top of my head. Like a banana being peeled, the light being unzipped a layer of my energetic field and pulled it off me.

As this happened, I felt an almost instant relief over my entire physical body and energetic being.

The light being had pulled off all the energetic density and debris that felt like it was suffocating me. All the energetic residue made me feel like I was covered in super glue, and it was gone in an instant. It was only then I really understood what the light being was there to help me with.

The light being left immediately after it removed my energetic casing, and I felt fantastic. I was so appreciative and grateful to Source. I couldn't believe how great I felt and how much I'd been suffering under the super glue-like energetic weight before that happened.

I sat there in bed in astonishment before lying down and falling asleep once more, feeling comfortable and finally completely at peace.

I'm not sure how long I slept before another interruption came to wake me up. Something new was trying to enter my body through my crown chakra and whatever it was, it did not feel like the same kind, loving energy of the light being who peeled my energy field.

A thought entered my awareness (it was a reminder of something I'd been told recently while doing my energy work). I remembered someone once told me it was a good idea to ask the question to those trying to gain access to your energy: Are you of the light and do you love me unconditionally?

So, I did.

When I asked this question, it was my "I AM Presence" who instantly came forward with a reply for me on my behalf. My head began to shake with a vigorous, emphatic, *No!*

I then immediately shook off whatever it was trying to gain access to my energy field and said, "I intend, you do *not* have my permission ever to enter my body or being or energy field."

I was amazed at how my head physically shook in answer to my posed question. It was reassuring to know an answer would always come to me, and help was always available to me when I needed it. Our "I AM Presence" is always serving our highest good if we ask, intend, and allow it to occur.

This experience helped me remember how to communicate more effectively with The Divine for my own benefit and highest good. I was able to receive direct, divine guidance, and I was blessed with the knowledge I AM never truly alone and The Divine always has my back because I intend it to be so.

I later found out from Archangel Raphael the beautiful light being was sent from Source to help me in my time of need.

Archangel Raphael also confirmed it was my "I AM Presence" who shook my head in answer to my question. This was a reminder my "I AM Presence" is ever present with me and assisting me as I intend it to be so, as we are one in the same. Archangel Raphael explained to me it was a being based in its own ego and had its own agenda that did not align with mine, who had tried to gain access to my energy field the second time. It was not a harmful being, it simply was not appropriate for me to engage with it for my own highest good at the time.

If asked, the answer from your "I AM Presence" will always ring true for you and resonate more powerfully than anything else. It is most beneficial for you, if you choose to ever rely on, turn to, and place all your attention on your own "Mighty I AM Presence," your source for your being and life, and to acknowledge and accept it as such. I have come to know absolutely every experience I have ever had in my life has been an opportunity for me. In the moment of each experience, I hold steadfast to the knowing, that my "I AM Presence" is my sole provider and my absolute source for every-thing, now and for all eternity itself sustained.

Honest as the day is long,
Try your best to be.
If you are choosing in this moment,
To be one with magnificent me.

Telling the truth,
Even when it's hardest to do.
This is what
I ask of you.

Seeing the light within yourself,
And within everything...
Well, that's what truly makes
My heart sing.

Telling yourself always,
Just how wonderful you truly are.
Well, by doing this, my beloved,
You will surely journey far.

With your hand on your heart,
Daily "I love yous" will set your heart aglow.
Then compassion and kindness,
The world will come to know.

I love you,
Your "I AM Presence."

TAKEAWAYS FOR YOUR TOOLBOX

The entire universe, which you are one with, loves you unconditionally beyond measure. It is always serving your highest good, even if you do not understand how that is occurring.

Every experience you have is a divine gift. It is all a matter of your perception. For example, if you experience a door closing, it only means there is something much better in store for you. We can perceive it as a loss, or we can choose to see the gift The Divine is offering us in that moment. Our role then becomes one of having absolute trust in The Divine, which in turn, allows the miracle to reveal itself in divine time and order. The Divine can help you if you have the courage to ask, and it will always look out for you, serving your highest good and the highest good of all, which you are one with.

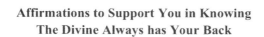

Affirmations to Support You in Knowing
The Divine Always has Your Back

I AM commanding, demanding, and intending, I AM the *Victory* of the oneness and the consciousness and the pure knowing, that absolutely everything and all is a divine blessing and gift for me at any given moment, now, continuously, and for all eternity itself sustained; so be it, and so it is.

I AM commanding, demanding, and intending, I AM the *Victory* of the oneness and the consciousness, and the pure knowing that my divine "Beloved I AM Presence" is always ever present with me. It is serving my absolute highest healing, highest good, highest outcome, and highest well-being at any given moment, all through pure unconditional love, and is always aligned with divine will and the purest, highest, greatest vibrational frequencies that possibly exist at any given moment; so be it, and so it is.

I AM commanding, demanding, and intending, I AM the *Victory* of always being in my "I AM Presence," and my "I AM Presence" is always within me; so be it, and so it is.

I AM commanding, demanding, and intending that I Am the *Victory* of always knowing that the universe always has my back, now and for all eternity itself sustained; so be it, and so it is.

I AM commanding, demanding, and intending, I AM the *Victory* of ever abiding in the light of my "Mighty I AM Presence," the highest, divine aspect of who it is that I AM; so be it, and so it is.

Chapter Nine

Love

*L*ove is everything in all of creation and existence. All that stems from Source is love, and by acting *in* and *as* love, you are acting as your true self—a divine being of pure unconditional love and light you are and have always been. Through understanding the laws of the universe, and acting in accordance with them, you will come to remember, know, and experience what it means to be in harmony with the entire universe. You will come to know what it means to be in harmony with yourself. You and the universe are one.

All is love, there is nothing else.

In love's heart,
Exists the All.
In love's heart,
You hear the call.

A calling to you,
That has always been,
And now you listen,
And thus begin.

To remember a time,
Not long ago,
When unity and oneness,
And abundance did flow.

A time so magnificent,
There are no words to be,
Just a time to remember,
When your heart was free.

So, blessed be you,
In your awakening to the All.
And know it is time,
For love has made its call.

TAKEAWAYS FOR YOUR TOOLBOX

Love is who you are. Love is who everything and everyone else is in all of creation and existence. There is nothing that is not love at its true, core essence. Love is always pure and harmonious in its divine perfection. Love does not seek for anything or strive to be anything; it is. Love is simple. Love is kind. Love is compassionate. Love is patient. Love is all good things now and forevermore.

I would say love is forgiving, except it does not ever need to be because, in love's eyes, all is always divine perfection. Therefore, there is absolutely nothing to forgive.

If you take a moment and choose to see through the eyes of love, through the eyes of your own "I AM Presence" how it sees you always as your divine self, instantaneous perfection can manifest.

We are all eternal love, playing in the realm of relativity, in this now moment. Love is always in command no matter what outer appearances may be, and all is truly well.

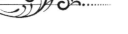

Affirmations to Remind You That
You Are Love

I AM commanding, demanding, and intending, I AM the *Victory* of pure unconditional love and light, wherever I abide, move, and go, now and for all eternity itself sustained; so be it, and so it is.

I AM commanding, demanding, and intending, I AM the *Victory* of the oneness, the consciousness, and the pure knowing that I AM pure unconditional love and light, and continuously I AM radiating, infinitely so, the divine, purest, highest, greatest vibrational frequencies possible, now and for all eternity itself sustained; so be it, and so it is.

I AM commanding, demanding, and intending, I AM the *Victory* of always being one with the divine miraculous; so be it, and so it is.

I AM commanding, demanding, and intending, I AM the *Victory* of calling upon now the Legions of the Angels of the Sacred Fire from the Great Central Sun, to come everywhere that sacred fire is needed in this whole world and in my whole world and establish it, now and for all eternity itself sustained, as the controlling power of this whole world, and as the controlling power of my whole world; so be it, and so it is.

I AM commanding, demanding, and intending that I AM the *Victory* of always loving, adoring, and cherishing myself, at any given moment, now, continuously, and for all eternity itself sustained as the absolute divine perfection that I AM; so be it and so it is.

Hold tight,
Be ever so still.
Have always faith,
In eternal divine will.

For your wishes,
Have been heard,
And are flowing back,
To you now.

Have trust, feel good,
To open and allow.

The mystery is deep,
No need to understand.
Just be in joy,
And all you will command.

Does it sound too simple?
Can this really be?
Oh, my beloved,
Give it a try now and see.

For, all the ingredients,
Listed above,
Are a brew for divine alchemy,
Delivered with love.

I love you.

Chapter Ten

Awareness

*O*nce you focus your attention on something and you become aware of focused attention, you will begin to see evidence of what you have chosen to place your focused attention on. You will begin to see more of it. This is known as synchronicity, being in the flow of life. Maintaining a mindset of openness, curiosity, and willingness is key.

At this stage of my journey, I found myself being present more often. I was coming to understand and truly know there were absolutely no coincidences in life, none. I had been through too many experiences that showed me otherwise.

I completed my courses and became certified in all three levels of Integrated Energy Therapy. I also furthered my education with the same instructor and became certified in Reiki.

Through my awakening, I was constantly immersed in helpful information. I was reminded everything dwells within us. We are infinite, divine wisdom and therefore we are not ever taught anything, instead, we are remembering divine wisdom has always been within. Through my own experiences, I feel the universe was, and still is, helping me to remember all things are possible through and with our Creator, who we are each one with in all ways, always.

Synchronicities became frequent in my life, and yet, they still managed to surprise me whenever they showed up. I am always quickly reminded, by The Divine, these synchronicities which we deem as miraculous, are the norm in *oneness*. I am reminded how we often, because so many of us have forgotten who we are, chalk these happenings up to either luck or a one-off miracle we can't seem to explain.

These miraculous instances can occur for us when we allow our hearts to open and when we allow ourselves to see the divinity and light within ourselves and within all things. Being one with the miraculous is our natural way of being when we aren't in a state of forgetfulness of who it is we truly are.

I was continuously witnessing clear evidence of miracles in my life, big and small, and I was truly grateful for each one of them. I found as I focused my attention on those synchronistic events appearing in my life, even more synchronistic events showed up for me. This is because we are powerful creators, and this is a universe of attraction, and what we place our attention on always expands.

Of course, remaining curious about life and allowing yourself to see through the eyes of a child, with childlike wonder and innocent perception, will enhance your life experience. It's all a matter of being receptive and present in each moment, which will enable you to recognize that divine gifts are always flowing to you from your Source, your own "I AM Presence."

Magic, magic, everywhere,
Is it real? Is it true?
Oh, dear one,
I leave that solely up to you.

Through eons of time,
As I do again right now,
I deliver my messages,
That I AM the way, and I AM the how.

Can you release your grip,
On what you believe is so real?
Can you let go now,
Without knowing the whole deal?

If you take that leap,
I will catch you in my heart,
For the truth is, dear one,
We have never been apart.

I had developed quite a healthy collection of beautiful crystals, purchasing them on my regular visits to my favorite holistic store. I had several books on crystals, and I felt a real connection to them. Soulutions had almost every type of crystal there was. If they didn't have it in stock, Honey could acquire it.

I knew most of the attributes of each crystal from my readings, and I often enjoyed learning about the new ascension crystals surfacing as the consciousness of humanity continued to rise.

I had placed several crystals in specific areas around my apartment and on my nightstand. My son even had a few crystals of his own he had picked out and placed around his room.

Once, I had to use the bathroom in the middle of the night. When I returned to my bed, the crystal, a piece of fluorite typically on my nightstand, had been moved into my bed. It was positioned right where the center of my back would be if I were to lie down.

At first, in all honesty, it shocked and scared me. I didn't know why it had been placed there and, more importantly to me, I didn't know *who* placed it there. I proceeded to put the crystal back on my nightstand and did my best to fall asleep.

Several nights passed by before it happened again.

I got up in the middle of the night to use the bathroom, and on my return to bed, there was a crystal lying right on top of my sheets. It was the same crystal, and it was placed in the same position on my bed.

I still do not know why the crystal kept finding its way to my bed every time I went to use the restroom. I looked up the meaning and some of the attributes of fluorite after that experience. I read fluorite cleanses and stabilizes the aura and can be used for protection.

I know everything has consciousness, including crystals, and they are all here to support us on our journeys if we ask and intend them to do so. I feel the fluorite crystal was placed there to serve my highest good for a benevolent reason.

Along my journey, I have come to know it serves one's highest good and the highest good of all to accept any divine gift, whatever it may be, from the heart, with appreciation and gratitude.

The Divine uses infinite avenues to deliver its messages to you at any given moment. In my personal experience, The Divine always knows what will capture my attention, for example, the use of number sequences.

When my awakening process first began, my son and I searched online to discover the spiritual meaning behind the number *1111*. We would often see these numbers on mailboxes, car license plates, digital clocks, and in many other places.

My son and I became caught up in our discovery of what was taking place. It took us about a month of seeing number sequences before we finally thought it might be a good idea to check online for the meaning of it all.

We found an article describing the meaning of the number *1111*. The online article explained it was the number sequence of awakening consciousness.

Seeing the number sequence *1111* is like an alarm clock of sorts. It is an alarm clock we each set for ourselves before incarnating. This alarm clock, the seeing of specific number sequences, is meant to remind each of us it is time to awaken from the dream. More specifically, it is time to awaken out of separation consciousness into the remembrance of oneness and the wholeness of divine perfection we have always been.

My son and I found this fascinating. The more we noticed the number sequences, the more they seemed to occur. This is because, once again, what we focus our attention on always expands.

One day, I drove to get something to eat with my son. My cell phone was resting on top of my console in my car as I drove. My cell phone began to beep sporadically. It was not ringing like it normally did, and it had no particular pattern to it.

My son and I looked quizzically at each other as we tried to come up with reasons and an explanation as to why my phone would be making these odd sounds. At first, a thought came to me: it may have been my uncle who had transitioned. I thought maybe it was his way of letting my son and me know he was okay, and all was well with him. It continued for several days.

Finally, it dawned on me to begin looking at the digital clock in my car or the clock in my home when the phone beeped. I began to write down the number sequences on the digital clock each time my phone beeped. Next, I went online to look for the meanings of these specific number sequences. It was then I found an amazing angel number site online.

I was fortunate to find a woman in Australia who channeled all the spiritual meanings for every possible number sequence into the thousands. I knew right away I had been led to that site by The Divine. It was then I realized The Divine was using these specific number sequences to deliver important messages to me.

I looked up all the number sequences and was in absolute awe of the actual conversations I was having with the divine angelic realm. The messages continued to come into my awareness frequently, and they always seemed to be spot-on regarding the information they were delivering at any given moment.

I had no doubt in my mind these specific divine messages were meant for me.

On one occasion, my son and I were driving to the beach, a two-hour drive from where we lived. My phone beeped the entire way down to the beach non-stop, with messages to me from the angels.

It happened so often I began to always carry a notebook with me. My son became a scribe, writing the numbers down as they were delivered. Most times, the messages through the number sequences came so quickly all we had time to do was write them down and save them to look up later.

I was wrapping a birthday gift on my bedroom floor one day. It was during the afternoon, and my son was busy doing homework in his bedroom. My cell phone began to beep sporadically once again. However, I did not get up immediately to answer it this time, as I was wanting to finish what I was doing. I heard my son yell out to me to answer my phone, the angels had a message for me. I asked my son if he could come and look at the number sequence. He said he was in the middle of doing something and he couldn't.

I decided to finish wrapping my gift and then I stood up to retrieve my phone from my nightstand. I wrote down the number on the digital clock and proceeded to go online to my angelic numbers site and look up its meaning. I read the message the angels were wanting me to receive, and I immediately began to laugh out loud. The message read, "We, the angelic realm, have been trying to get your attention for the longest time!"

I quickly yelled for my son and shared the message with him, and we both had a good laugh. I said to him, "No one would ever believe this even if we told them." It was another divine gift, and I was so grateful for it.

My phone continued to beep, delivering angelic messages through numeric sequences, for the better part of a year. The messages were always encouraging and based in love. It was pure, true, divine guidance, and I was grateful for the gift.

I feel and know from my own experiences it is truly divine magic we are remembering. We are remembering the realms of magic are our true home and is the place we are returning to.

This world we are in, as beautiful and as awe-inspiring and amazing as it is, is the dream. We are each waking from the dream to the pure divine magic, the pure love, we have always been. The more we allow ourselves to love our own hearts, the more our true home can reveal itself to us.

That journey is occurring now for each of us if we choose. It is a journey filled with the remembrance of pure joy, bliss, and eternal light. It is a destination you have always been but may have forgotten. All it takes is a remembrance of All That Is that dwells within, along with loving self and all things and all others as self, for it to be revealed to you in the Now. It is a continuous journey into your heart where it all begins and ends and starts. You are infinite and eternal divine love.

The mind is constantly seeking control of things. Answers are needed by the mind in order to do that, but the heart never questions. There is an innate trust that stems from the heart through the infinite wisdom of love. So, it is important to become aware of your questioning so you can drop down into your knowing and trusting space instead.

The Divine was always in my awareness. I would find crystals randomly laying around on the floor of my apartment, mostly in front of doorways where I would have to step over the crystal in order to pass by.

I believe the reason they were frequently placed in front of a doorway was to grab my attention. In this way, I would be sure not to miss them. I also feel it was The Divine's way of communicating to me I am never, ever alone.

One day, I found a shiny penny on the floor inside the front door of my apartment on the day of my son's eighth-grade graduation. At that moment, I intuitively knew it was my biological mother saying hello. I knew she was letting me know she was going to be present at my son's graduation.

My intuition was getting more powerful and the synchronicities occurring in my life were on the upswing.

One evening, as I was beginning to fall asleep, I heard the most enchanting melodies.

At first, I thought it might have been my son, so I decided to get out of bed and have a good look around the apartment. I walked into my son's room, and I saw he was fast asleep. I walked back toward my room and could not hear anything at all.

I walked into the kitchen to get a glass of water. As I was opening the refrigerator door, the angelic music began, and it was even louder this time. I immediately froze, trying to be silent to hear as much of the music as I could.

It sounded like a symphony with a choir of angelic singing voices accompanying it.

After several minutes had passed, the melodies stopped playing, and I decided to walk back to my room and go back to sleep.

Hearing angelic music happened again and again in the days that followed. Because I was tuned into my surroundings and open to the magic, I was able to bring an awareness to the angelic choir which had likely been there the whole time. I simply couldn't hear it because I wasn't paying enough attention.

As you look for divine magic,
It looks for you too.
Peeking through dimensions,
Its love shines through.

A flash of light,
And a… "What was that?" you say,
Just little dear ones, my love,
Coming to play.

Hoping you remember,
A love so true.
Hoping to be seen,
As pure love by you.

Beautiful ones of great power,
They truly are.
Not so very near,
Yet, not so very far.

Held in a space,
That only pure love can see.
Calling them in now,
With your happiness and glee.

I started volunteering at my favorite spiritual store, Soulutions for Daily Living, and I was still attending monthly channeling sessions with Kelly Kolodney and Archangel Raphael for divine guidance.

I was also attending my regular, monthly doctor appointments with the hopes of reducing my medications. I was doing well, and I finally reached a point where I was able to wean myself off all medications. I was able to accomplish this without having my temperature spike or the disease becoming active once again. My doctor was pleased with my positive results, and I was too.

Because I'd been having healing interactions with The Divine, I knew they were working through me, healing and detoxing my body, and getting rid of all traces of the medication from my system. The medication took two years to completely flush out of my body.

I had been on steroids for almost twenty years. I truly feel and know my complete healing had everything to do with the decision I made that day in my apartment while listening to the song "Save Your Life" by The Newsboys.

It was the decision to follow the light and align myself with my "I AM Presence," my divine purpose, and it consequently altered the course of my life. I chose the light in that moment as I was listening to the message being delivered to me through the lyrics of the song.

I feel I am doing my best to not only live, but also to thrive. With my pure intent, I am continuously aligning myself with my highest timeline, my highest resonance and light, the fullness of all I have become, my "Beloved I AM Presence."

The choice we are each gifted by The Divine is our free will, the choice of choosing love, or not, in each now moment. The divine blessing is that this gift is available to us right now. It is The Divine's ultimate invitation. It is an extended hand always outstretched to you waiting for you to grab ahold of it. It is a "come as you are" invitation, and the invitation is always being offered.

Hop to the highest timeline,
Ah! I am already there.
Oh, this is fun.
Without a moment to spare.

To be or not to be?
This is my choice-filled life.
Glide I do through this beautiful realm,
Without any stress or strife.

It's all your choice you see…
You choose all you wish to be.
So, take this moment and cease the dos,
Take this moment,
And begin to choose.

Let it all come to you…
For I tell you, it surely will.
All it takes is knowing who you are,
And being ever so still.

You are Master.

So many amazing and magical occurrences took place for me while I was volunteering at Soulutions for Daily Living.

One day, I decided to buy a selenite crystal, known for its many divine healing properties. Some of these properties include connecting to the third eye, crown, and etheric chakras. Selenite, through radiating light energy, is said to promote purity and honesty.

Honey keeps the crystals in glass jars so her customers can see which crystals they are picking from the many available. I lifted a glass, which was full of small selenite crystals, and I decided to reach into the bottom of the glass jar and pull out one selenite crystal.

Honey was sitting at the register. I handed her the crystal I had selected to purchase, and as I did, I glanced down at the crystal for the first time. I noticed something inside of it, and I asked Honey to wait before ringing up my purchase as I began to study the crystal closely. I could not believe what I was seeing.

Inside the crystal, as clear as day, was my initial, "K" for Kim. There was no mistaking it. It was in the dead center of the selenite crystal.

Honey proceeded to examine the crystal as well. Both of our mouths hung wide open in astonishment upon that wondrous discovery. I believe Honey was accustomed to bearing witness to daily miracles that always seemed to occur at her store and this was no exception.

I paid for the crystal, and when I returned home, the first thing I did was show my son the beautiful gift I had received from The Divine that day. It was another reminder I was on my path, in the flow, and all was truly well.

Fairy dust, starlight,
And twinkles divine…
Oh, how I love,
A magical time.

Mystical invitations,
To playtime and more…
Bliss, joy, and happiness,
Allow hearts to soar.

For the wishing well is infinite,
No bottom to be found,
And therein lies your dreams,
Where all your wishes abound.

So, play along, won't you now,
In this eternal game divine.
Find what lights you up,
And be it all the time.

For as you feel good,
Allowing your heart to glow…
Your innermost Merlin,
You will surely come to know.

It was a sunny day, and the crispness of fall was in the air.

My son was on the tennis team at his school, and he brought a friend home to play a game or two on the courts in our complex. Lucky for me, our apartment was positioned in full view of all the tennis courts, and I was able to watch the boys play from my apartment patio.

I walked with the boys to the tennis courts that day to make sure they were able to get in without any problems. To our luck, the tennis court's gates were unlocked, and the boys were able to begin their game. I walked back to my apartment and found a comfortable chair to sit on to view the game.

Toward the end of the boys' match, I saw something had captured their attention. I was not close enough to hear what the boys were speaking about, but I was sure I would soon find out.

"Mom, you gotta see this!" my son said as he flew through the door to our apartment after his match. "Look what I found!"

When he came over to me, there was a blue paperclip in the shape of a guitar sitting in the palm of his hand.

"Oh, that's amazing. Where'd you find that?" I asked.

He said, "So, I went to play, right, and there wasn't anything around and no one came by while we were out there. I put my bag down, and we had our game."

I agreed since I'd been sitting on the balcony watching them.

"Well, I went to get a drink from the water bottle which was right next to my bag, and this was resting right next to it."

I glanced at the paperclip again.

"I would have seen it when I first put my bag down and got my water bottle out. This isn't even close to the same color as the court. There's no way anyone could have placed it there without us noticing," he explained.

We all nodded in agreement no one could have snuck onto the court without us noticing them.

"Mom," he said, "I think I'm supposed to learn how to play the guitar."

Having had all the amazing experiences I'd already had with The Divine, I knew and, more importantly, felt what my son was saying was true. I thought to myself, *It's most definitely time to look for a guitar instructor.*

I enrolled my son in after-school guitar lessons a week or so after he had found the blue paperclip next to his tennis bag. He absolutely loved playing the guitar and learned it rather quickly.

My son ended up stopping his in-person guitar lessons, and he began tutoring himself with online courses instead. This option made it easier for my son to learn at his own pace, which better suited his schedule.

I kept the small, royal blue paper clip as my son's gift from The Divine and later had it framed for him.

My son has used his story, the finding of the magical, royal blue paperclip, on several occasions throughout his life. One of those occasions was in his admissions essay for college. The college replied with an acceptance for my son, and a special note inside saying how much the admissions' staff had enjoyed reading the story of my son finding the mysterious paperclip.

The color of the paperclip, royal blue, I feel is also significant, as is everything divine. Royal blue, some say, is known to be the color of spirit. I think it manifested for my son, in that specific color so my son would have no doubt whatsoever as to who the giver of the gift had been.

My son is now a country music artist. He attended college in Nashville, Tennessee, where he lives today. He loves what he does, and he is following his divine purpose, his dreams, which are, for him, one and the same.

Before the royal blue paperclip appeared to my son, he had never picked up an instrument other than in music class in school. He certainly did not think of himself as a musician prior to finding the paperclip.

Without that gift, I am almost certain the guitar lessons would have never occurred.

It is why it is so important to live in the Now. It is so important to be fully present so you can see, hear, and perceive with all your senses all the amazing messages and gifts The Divine is always sending your way.

Divine messages are always flowing to you. The important question to ask yourself is: *Am I allowing myself to receive them?*

If you find yourself worrying over the past, or having anxiety over what is yet to unfold, you miss the signs The Divine is sending you in the present moment. These are the signs of your purpose. These divine signs are always present to show you the way for your highest good and the highest good of all.

Therefore, enjoying, and being grateful for where you are right now, and being in full acceptance of how life is showing up for you in each moment, is the key to happiness.

If my son had not been fully present, he would have more than likely missed seeing the paperclip sitting next to his bag. Or, if he did happen to see it, he probably would not have recognized it as a divine sign. Instead, he may have thought it was a mere coincidence.

However, I know through my own experiences there are absolutely no coincidences in life. None.

Even if you happen to get stung by a bee, there is a reason for it. You may never know the reason, but there is one. Everything is energy and everything is connected. You are always emitting a frequency, and whatever frequency you are emitting at any given moment, you are attracting experiences into your life matching that same frequency.

Look closely, deeply
And ever so clear.
For in truth,
There is only one of us here.

Shoulder to shoulder you stand,
With the Great Masters of Light.
For if you place them on a pedestal of oneness,
You then lose sight.

Honoring the divinity,
Within the one and the All,
Seeing each as equal, none grand or small.
This beloved is the key to it all.

Celebrate all you love,
That you may see in another.
They are so much more,
Than a sister or a brother.

They are all you,
Now and forevermore...
And what you bestow upon them,
You bestow upon self for sure.

Loving all as self with compassion,
I pray you choose to be...
For I, we, them, that, there, and those,
It's all me.

We are one.

During my individual sessions with Divine Archangel Raphael, the angel recommended several books for me to read to facilitate the expansion of my consciousness.

On many occasions, I saw sparkles of light literally jump off the pages I was reading. This was a joy to me because it offered yet another confirmation, although it was not needed; these pages were filled with divine sacred light codes to assist me on my journey.

One book that changed my life forever, in numerous, magnificent ways was *Conversations with God* by Neale Donald Walsch.

At one point, I was a bit stumped on some universal truths. I had not quite grasped how the universal laws operated, and I was still seeking answers from the external at this stage. I can tell you my requests were heard and answered by The Divine, through the reading of this book.

I went to my local grocery store one day. I pulled into the parking lot and parked directly behind a car that had a plethora of spiritual bumper stickers on its back window. I entered the store and grabbed a shopping cart and was on my way.

I went straight to the produce section, and it was there I met a lovely woman. We struck up a conversation almost immediately. We spoke first about the food choices available, discussing whether they were organic. Then, our conversation somehow took a turn, and we began speaking to each other about our favorite books. It was then the woman suggested I read *Conversations with God* by Neale Donald Walsch.

I told her I had a backlog of books to read, and I would most certainly add it to my list. She then persisted in suggesting the book to me once again. She told me when she read the book it helped her tremendously.

I thanked her and continued with my shopping. Just as I was leaving the parking lot of the grocery store, I saw the same woman getting into the car parked directly in front of me with the multitude of spiritual bumper stickers.

I was aware of the synchronicity of the entire event and made a mental note to purchase the book. I knew The Divine, *a.k.a. me,* wanted me to read it.

I did not know how helpful that book would be for me. Two more people suggested that same book to me within three weeks' time. After I read the book, I found it had answered almost every question I had been wondering about that I could not seem to piece together on my own. The Divine had delivered to me exactly what I needed when I needed it.

To this day, I often use *Conversations with God* as a reference. I keep it by my bedside, and I often get a nudge to open it up to a random page, which, by the way, is *never random.* The messages are always exactly what I need to hear exactly when I need to hear them, and I am grateful.

Seeing with only eyes for light,
I allow my soul to take flight.
Guidance within is all around.
Magical messages are easily found.

The bright moon is my reminder,
To have no despair,
For the light in its infiniteness,
Is everywhere.

Bathe yourself in this knowing,
Be comforted this night.
Be one with the moon,
And its luminous light.

For all is teacher,
And the moon is too.
It says, "Even in the darkest night,
The light shines through."

All is well.

TAKEAWAYS FOR YOUR TOOLBOX

On my journey, I have come to remember time does not exist. It has been created by the human collective, giving us, through the gift of our senses, the opportunity to move through this Earth realm and experience all the rich tapestry it has to offer. The past does not exist, and the future is yet to be birthed, so we truly have only this present moment.

I have found worrying about a past that no longer exists and having anxiety of what is still yet to come is wasted energy. The only time that exists is this present moment. This is where all your power is because *the now* is the moment where all decisions are made. In most cases, if you were to stop briefly and quiet yourself, and take inventory of how you are feeling in this moment, more than likely, you would discover all is well with you. It is the mind, the ego, ruminating on a past that no longer exists, and who likes to bring forth anxiety about a situation not even showing itself to be true yet.

We are each such powerful Master Creators, whether we are conscious of truth or not.

When you dwell on a past that does not exist (and since you are constantly creating your own reality), you tend to recreate it over and over. When you have anxiety about what is yet to come to fruition, you are focusing on that outcome, and more than likely bring it forth into your experience. This is because this is where you are placing your attention, and where attention is placed creates more of that which we are focused upon.

Living in the present moment, in awareness, requires full faith and trust in the universe. You are the universe and therefore, you will always provide for yourself. However, as long as one is living in a nonexistent past and a nonexistent future, that cannot occur. The only reason someone is likely to dwell on the past and worry about the future is because they somehow feel they are alone and will not be provided for by the universe.

The universe only has one answer for you always, and that answer is *yes*. Therefore, when you surrender and trust and have faith in the universe—which is, in truth, you—you are always provided for in all ways. Therefore, many people choose to take up the practice of meditation. It helps you to quiet your mind and gain control of your thoughts. It assists you in living in the present moment. Then, from this space of having a still mind, you can focus your thoughts and place your attention on, and choose to co-create the outcomes that you desire.

Meditation also can take many forms. It doesn't have to be sitting in a room and being quiet. Taking a walk can be a meditation. Cooking can be a form of meditation. Anything you enjoy and requires you to still your mind and focus on the present moment is very helpful.

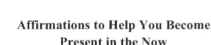

Affirmations to Help You Become
Present in the Now

I AM intending, commanding, and demanding that I AM always the *Victory* of being present and conscious in each now moment; so be it, and so it is.

I AM intending, commanding, and demanding, I AM the *Victory* of being grounded, tethered, and anchored into the iron core of Mother Earth, in the New Earth, now, continuously, and for all eternity itself sustained; so be it, and so it is.

I AM intending, commanding, and demanding that I AM the *Victory* of God Source Consciousness; I AM always living for the world, and I AM always choosing to be now. The eternal now, is the only time that exists, and I AM surrendering to this now present moment where it is I AM, with deep gratitude and appreciation to my "Mighty I AM Presence" for this magnificent gift now and for all eternity itself sustained; so be it, and so it is.

I AM intending, commanding, and demanding that I AM the *Victory* of always being right where I AM meant to be, for all is always in divine perfect time and order; so be it, and so it is.

I AM intending, commanding, and demanding that I AM so grateful that in this now present moment all is well with me in all ways, always; so be it, and so it is.

I AM intending, commanding, and demanding that I AM always the *Victory* of being safe, capable, and lovable, now, continuously, and for all eternity itself sustained; so be it, and so it is.

Chapter Eleven

Compassion

ncle George experienced a rapid decline in his health when my son and I moved into our new apartment. Even though I spent most of my days clearing energetic debris and density from my field, I did my best to visit him at his home daily.

He was on oxygen, and it was becoming difficult for him to walk. He had a stair lift to take him to the top of the stairs where his bedroom was located. However, due to his shortness of breath, getting himself to the stair lift was becoming a difficult process for him.

At one o'clock in the morning, my son came into my room urging me to wake up. As soon as he entered my room, I heard a loud banging from inside my apartment. It sounded like someone banging pots and pans together.

I climbed out of bed, and he followed me down the hallway which led to the kitchen, where we discovered not only were the pots and pans being banged together, but we could also hear the cabinet doors being opened and slammed shut.

My son was calmer than I was in the face of all the ruckus, but neither of us wanted to get super close to the kitchen.

I wondered, *What now?* I couldn't tell what the being wanted once it had our full attention, but I had the feeling it didn't want to hurt us.

"What do we do, Mom? What's causing this?" my son asked.

As soon as he asked, a thought of Uncle George came into my awareness. I had an intuitive feeling something had happened to him.

The longer my son and I discussed what we should do, the louder and more urgent the banging became. I decided to call my cousin who had been with me when we had the encounter with our departed relatives at my aunt's house.

Of course, it was not the norm for me to be up in the middle of the night, let alone calling someone at that time, but my cousin picked up her phone, thankfully.

"Hello?" she answered.

"Hey, so you know how we've had interactions with light beings before? Well, one of them is here now, and I don't know if you can hear it, but it's making a ton of noise in my kitchen right now. I wondered if you had any suggestions," I said.

My cousin paused to think for a moment, and I couldn't blame her. I'd likely woken her up, so it was reasonable she'd need time to focus.

Finally, she suggested, "Have you tried asking it to leave?"

I hadn't, so I directed my attention to the being in the kitchen again and said, "I intend, command, and demand whoever is causing all of the commotion in my kitchen right now to leave my apartment immediately."

Everything stopped and it became quiet instantly, but before I could feel true relief, loud knocking began on my front door.

I was exasperated. I thought, *This must be some sort of joke!* However, I knew better than that.

I wasn't specific enough in my request for the being to leave my son and me alone for the night. Because I'd told it to leave my apartment instead of the entire apartment complex, it was still able to hold our attention by banging on my front door.

I was at my wit's end, and the whole situation had me in a tizzy. As this was occurring, it came into my awareness that the being banging the pots and pans was my Aunt Sallie, Uncle George's wife, who had already transitioned. Because I was informed by my "I AM Presence" that it was my aunt, I started to calm down a bit.

My son and I made the decision not to call my uncle because, by this time, it was already into the early hours of the morning. I didn't want to wake up my uncle and cause him alarm, if, in fact, I was incorrect in my assumptions regarding the entire situation.

I do not think my son and I got an ounce of sleep that night. The knocking on the front door of my apartment stopped immediately after my son and I spoke together about our plans for the following day. I intended to visit my uncle early the next day to see if he was all right and I somehow knew my aunt was aware of that decision and was at peace with it.

The next day, I drove my son to school and then headed straight down to my uncle's house to check on him.

I knocked on his front door and he answered. I brought him a chicken pot pie for lunch—one of his favorites—and we sat down together on the sofa to have a chat. It was hard for him to speak, but fortunately, I was able to understand him.

"Uncle George, did anything out of the ordinary happen last night?" I asked, not wanting to beat around the bush.

He nodded, explaining, "Yes. I didn't have the energy to go upstairs, but I decided to go anyway, and I fell in the process."

"Do you know what time it happened? Perhaps around one o'clock in the morning?"

He nodded again.

I knew instantly what I had surmised was true. My aunt, knowing my uncle had taken a fall, was doing her best to get my attention to have me help him in some way.

I proceeded to tell my uncle all about what had occurred the previous night. I explained it was his wife, Aunt Sallie, banging pots and pans and slamming cabinet doors and then finally knocking on my front door to get my attention to help him.

My uncle, having never been spiritual a day in his life to my knowledge, somehow understood what I was saying and smiled and nodded his head in agreement.

He then said, "I often feel Sallie's presence around me. I know she's here watching over me."

I could see the information I had given him had made him happy and had given him an overall sense of peace, which made me feel better about sharing it with him.

All the transcendental occurrences I had experienced up until this point were new to me when they took place. This latest experience was no exception, and I was having outer-worldly experiences almost daily.

I have come to know and believe the entire universe is love and is light and is always serving our highest good and the highest good of all simultaneously. However, during the first couple of years of my awakening process, these experiences were profound and a bit jarring to me.

Initially, I was not aware of how the universe operated. I was not aware of the universal laws always at play. I have since come to relax into the pure knowing of the love I AM and we all are, and I am so grateful for the wisdom I have acquired along my journey. I know when I hear a *bump in the night*, it is benevolent, and it is always here to assist me because I intend it to be so as the creator I AM.

I have come to know and truly believe I AM divine perfection, and all existence and creation is divine perfection as well. I have come to the realization I AM one with all creation and divine perfection at any given moment, and all is a divine, glorious, joyous, magnificent celebration of that. It is a trusting of divine love that evolves into a pure knowing through your own experience.

It is truly a blessing,
When a soul is set free.
No more pain, worry, or tears,
Can ever be.

It is a soul's instant relief,
A freedom, a pure bliss,
And for those left behind,
A knowing they could easily miss.

So, cry your tears,
Each and every one,
Then focus all your attention,
On the beauty that has begun.

For there is no strife,
Where this soul calls home.
Only love, light and freedom,
To forever roam.

He is welcomed lovingly,
By those that have gone before,
And only joy, love, and laughter is left,
For a heart that can now soar.

One morning, I received a call from my uncle. At this point, he could not speak at all. He mumbled over the phone to me, doing his best to form words, but I could not understand him.

I had visited him the day before, and we had lunch together in his kitchen. Once again, he ate his favorite chicken pot pie and seemed content. While my uncle and I were eating at his kitchen table, Aunt Sallie walked up to the table in her light body. I was so surprised I could see her.

She appeared as white light in the shape of a human body. She stood upright between my uncle and me.

I said, "Aunt Sallie is here."

My uncle turned and looked directly at my aunt, his wife, and said to her, "I am ready Sallie."

I did my best to hold back my tears as we finished our lunch together. That was the last time I saw him.

The next morning, after a brief phone conversation with my uncle, I immediately drove down to his home to check on him. I had a feeling he had already transitioned as I pulled up to his home. I got out of my car and walked to his front door. I proceeded to knock on his door and there was no answer.

I decided to call the police station, and they were able to enter his home through a small window. They told me they found my uncle lying on the floor and he had been grasping his cell phone. The police thought he was possibly trying to call for help.

I explained to the police their assumption was not the case. I made them aware that my uncle and I had recently gotten off the phone with each other, and he had called me to say goodbye.

Later that week, some relatives and I entered my uncle's home to start clearing things out. In the space above where the police had told me he had collapsed, there was a beautiful, vertically positioned, white light. I was comforted when I saw this light and I knew he was fine. I knew he and my aunt were together once again.

We are each loved unconditionally beyond measure by The Divine, who we are also one with, now and forevermore. These divine messages of love and light and of divine assistance are always available to each of us if we allow ourselves to open up and receive them.

Eyes wide awake,
Seeing only through your heart.
Focused attention on your desire,
You begin, end, and start.

The highest priority always,
Should you choose it to be…
Alignment with all you have become,
All you have become through me.

For your loving heart is the doorway,
To every treasure you seek,
And being one with feeling good,
Allows you to take a peek.

A peek into a reality,
That shows it to be true,
A plethora of well-being,
I only flow to you.

And as your doorway opens,
A little more each now.
You remember all once forgotten,
Of All That Is, you allow.

My son enjoyed being involved in theater when he was in high school. One of the plays he took part in was a production of *Alice in Wonderland*.

My son was sick the week prior to the play that was to be performed on an upcoming Friday evening. He was running a low-grade fever; however, he insisted on partaking in the play. Unfortunately, the teacher had no understudy for his role.

He went on and did a wonderful job, but I could see he was suffering through it.

After the play, my son explained to me he had been about to go on and perform his lines when he began to have a coughing fit backstage. He was in a panic, trying to decide whether he was going to be able to go on and perform his lines.

At that moment, my son glanced down at the stage floor. Lying on the floor, as he described it to me, directly in front of where my son was standing was a cough drop. My son said it was in a wrapper, and it appeared to have been placed there, directly on his path so he would not miss it.

He knew, in that instant, it had been a gift from The Divine.

My son told me there was absolutely no way he would have made it through his lines without that lozenge. The Divine knew this, too, and had compassion for his plight, thus deciding to help him.

It was yet another reminder for me and for my son all things are possible through and with our magnificent Creator. The Divine is always serving our highest good and always has our back if we intend it to be so.

Allowing your heart to open with kindness and compassion for yourself and for all else is the key to your happily ever after.

Compassion is the only way,
For a soul that has been set free.
Awake in the oneness in which it swims,
That is only what can be.

With eyes for only love and beauty,
Seeing each moment anew,
That beautiful soul now knows,
What is forever true.

That there is no separation,
No, no separation at all.
And when you are kind to another,
Only blessings upon you do fall.

So, swim in the ocean of oneness,
And see each moment anew,
And then begin to watch miraculously,
As all the wishes you've dreamed come true.

TAKEAWAYS FOR YOUR TOOLBOX

Compassion comes forth when we see through the lens of our "I AM Presence."

Love is who we each are at our core, our essence. When you live consciously and know you are love, that you are The Creative Source of All That Is, you are one with all things, compassion is a given. There would never again be another war of any kind, whether it be on an individual or global scale, if we all remembered who we truly are. With the remembrance of oneness, one would begin to treat all others and all things as self with deep compassion.

When you are love, you always have compassion for All That Is. You have great compassion for all living things as well as all non-living things. This is because you remember, and you realize they are all you. How would one treat someone if they knew it was literally them? Most likely, with great kindness and compassion.

People want what they want because they feel they would experience the feeling of happiness in the attainment of whatever it is they are seeking. We all want to feel happiness and to love and to be loved. We all want others to always be compassionate with us. Therefore, this compassion we are all desiring, which is really a great love for self, must come first from within. Since everything in the external world is a reflection of what you have going on inside of you, compassion, happiness, and love all must come from within. It must come from being compassionate, happy, and loving, first and foremost, to yourself. Then, when you are kind and compassionate with yourself, when you are happy just to be happy, and when you are fully loving who you are in full acceptance of yourself, you will experience this in your external life.

It all begins with you. It begins with knowing you are one with all things. The compassion component begins when you start to see yourself in others. You no longer see them as separate from yourself and this is where the deep compassion seeps in. This is when your heart opens wide and not only are you able to give great compassion to others, but in giving, since you are one with everything and all, you are at the same time receiving this great compassion you are giving. In the giving, you are receiving it for yourself. There is no separation, you are One with all things.

If you choose, you can begin to play the *I AM Here and I AM There* game, brought into my awareness by the Ascended Masters of Light. This game helps you to remember and to conceptualize that everything in your life is you. When you go about your day, you can point to yourself and say, "I AM here, and I AM also there," as you point to different objects. This helps you to remember and be conscious and present in the knowing that everything you are seeing through your eyes is you. It supports you to live once again in unity consciousness, on the New Earth, and leave separation consciousness behind, once and for all.

Affirmations to Assist in Opening Your Heart to Live with Great Compassion Not Only for Self but for All as We Are One

I AM intending, commanding, and demanding, I AM the *Victory* of always being one with my open, pure, grateful heart, that I AM always anchored and centered in; so be it, and so it is.

I AM intending, commanding, and demanding, I AM always the *Victory* of being a clear, sentient being of pure unconditional love and light, and I AM always radiating love and light infinitely so for the well-being of all that I AM now; so be it, and so it is.

I AM intending, commanding, and demanding, I AM the *Victory* of always loving, adoring, and cherishing myself as the absolute divine perfection I AM; so be it, and so it is.

I AM intending, commanding, and demanding, I AM the *Victory* of being loving and compassionate with myself, and others are always loving and compassionate with me; so be it, and so it is.

I AM intending, commanding, and demanding, I AM the *Victory* of always loving and accepting myself as the divine perfection that I AM right now, continuously, and for all eternity itself sustained; so be it, and so it is.

I AM intending, commanding, and demanding, I AM the *Victory* of awakening each day, one with divine clarity and an open heart, and I AM always eager for the day, fully merged with, aligned with and attuned to my "I AM Presence"; so be it, and so it is.

I AM intending, commanding, and demanding, I AM the *Victory* of always being divinely guided by the light in my heart; so be it, and so it is.

I AM intending, commanding, and demanding, I AM the *Victory* of being divinely guided by my "Mighty I AM Presence," and I AM always choosing to follow the divine guidance of my "Mighty I AM Presence" now, continuously, and for all eternity itself sustained; so be it, and so it is.

Chapter Twelve

Transcendental Experiences

My health, at this point, was divine perfection. I was healthy in all ways. It was as if I had never been ill. I was, however, still clearing density and having regular monthly appointments with Divine Archangel Raphael, which was extremely helpful with my ascension process.

Divine messages and transcendental experiences were on a continuous upswing for both my son and me. I was attending many workshops, and I was researching everything related to spirituality. I had a great interest in remembering as much as I could about the Divine Angelic Realm and the Divine Ascended Masters of Light.

This was a natural course for me because most of my experiences involved the angels and the Ascended Masters of Light, specifically Divine Archangel Raphael, Divine Archangel Michael, and Ascended Master Yeshua. I knew there were also many other Ascended Light Beings assisting me, but these aspects of divinity were the main ones I was interacting with.

Divine guidance is quantum,
Linear it is not.
Pay close attention,
To flashes of thought.

For it is within the imagination,
That your "I AM Presence" speaks to you.
It is also where you feel,
The love from too.

There is a system of love in place now,
That has your back, it's clear.
All things conceived in compassion and unity,
Will succeed, so have no fear.

So, try things again,
That may have not worked before.
The new energy is here to support you,
Of that you can be sure.

Both my son and I had our awakenings almost simultaneously. It was wonderful and comforting to have someone to share my outer-worldly experiences with and someone who understood completely because these experiences, although unique to each of us, were happening for him as well. It made it even more special for me as it was my son.

My son is an old soul. I have always felt he was wise beyond his years.

We are all ancient and timeless, as we are all one with The Creative Source; however, I believe my son has experienced many lifetimes here on Earth.

A whole new perspective was continuously opening to me, and I was discovering new truths almost every day about a reality I thought to be so steadfast and true. I found it fascinating. I was on an adventure of a lifetime, and this was just the beginning.

Naked feet dance,
On the earthen floor…
Pounding and beating,
Again, once more.

A dance of the ancients,
Of long ago,
Flashes and inklings,
Of once we did know.

Another space,
Where we moved before,
A space we create,
Again, once more…

To awaken a melody,
So deep within,
A powerful stirring,
We now begin.

A pounding and beating,
On the earth so deep,
With each step the light,
In our hearts does seep.

This dance is of the sacred,
This dance is of the pure,
This is the dance eternal,
And for love, we dance once more.

The Divine delivers many messages to us while we sleep. During this time, all energetic momentum subsides. Dreamtime is a space where we can receive divine messages easily without resistance. It is a space where our own minds are quieted, allowing for the whispers of Source, our own "I AM Presence," to connect with us on many levels. This is a space where deep healing can and often does occur.

I have had many amazing experiences during my dream state. In one of those dreams, I had the opportunity to meet a family member I had never really known on Earth. It was my sister, Robin.

My sister transitioned when I was very young, just two years of age. One evening, I found myself lucid in the middle of a dream. I was standing near a makeup counter in what appeared to be a mall. It was a busy scene. There were many people bustling around the area where I was standing.

I looked up and saw my sister directly in front of me. She was an adult in my lucid dream and much like I would have pictured her if she were alive today.

In my lucid dream, as soon as I saw my sister, our eyes locked, and I opened my arms to embrace her. She was so beautiful.

I said, "Hello, how have you been? It's so nice to see you!"

She said, "I am fine, how are you?"

I told her I was well, and it was so nice to meet her in the way we were meeting.

She nodded in agreement and after our brief embrace, she went on her way. After my sister had left me, I decided to purchase a lipstick. The salesperson informed me I did not have to pay for it. She even laughed at me because I thought I had to pay for the item. I woke up having many questions I was wanting answered.

My next scheduled session with Divine Archangel Raphael was filled with answers from the angel.

I asked Divine Archangel Raphael, "Why didn't I have to pay for anything in the store where I was with my sister? What realm was that?"

The angel answered, "It's a reality that is a notch above Earth, where you are now."

I, in turn, told the angel the woman working at the makeup counter in my dream said everything was free in that realm.

Archangel Raphael agreed and confirmed that to be true.

I thought, *Well what am I doing on Earth in this reality? If there's a realm where everything's free, I think I'd prefer that!* I then had a good laugh about it all. I was being shown by The Divine all is truly well. Our loved ones, even though they are not here in this reality with us anymore, are absolutely fine.

I was also being shown different realms and ways of being. I was being shown universal truths, one of which is that there are, in fact, many other dimensions and realms in existence. The lucid dream also brought into my awareness we are each in many, if not all, of those other realms simultaneously, even while we are here incarnated on Earth. I was being shown we truly are infinite.

Rips in the fabric,
Of time and space.
I peer into,
This magical place.

All eyes wide open,
With a heart that can see,
This enchanting realm,
Of possibility...

That begs to be witnessed,
And now to be seen.
With just one whisper,
I hear it scream.

"We are here.
So close, yet so very far...
Travel through your heart to me,
It is your guiding star."

So many synchronicities began to come into my awareness at this stage of my journey. There were so many it is difficult to remember them all. On several different occasions, I fell asleep and experienced white angel feathers falling into my mouth out of nowhere. I smelled flowers carried by the wind under my nose.

I would watch television and receive specific divine guidance, uttered out of the mouths of actors on the screen. So many messages were, and still are, delivered to me from The Divine through songs, aromas, numbers, books, and from the comments of other people to name a few. Whatever will catch your attention the universe tends to use. I often receive many of what you might call "downloads." This is information I receive from The Divine that, with my intention, is always aligned with divine, pure, unconditional love.

The term *download* is a metaphor used to explain the process of receiving an influx of knowledge, higher light frequencies, or consciousness updates to your mental and physical systems. The information is then stored within you for you to use whenever it is the divine perfect time to do so.

For example, I received a download for this book I am writing several years ago. On several different occasions, I also remember The Divine flicking the lights on and off in my kitchen to get my attention and to inform me a download was imminent. Whenever this occurred, I knew it was time for me to go lie down to receive.

Sometimes, extreme fatigue comes over me in an instant. I know it is also The Divine purposely making me tired so I will go and lie down. I surrender to divine will and then The Divine comes in and proceeds to do whatever is needed for my highest good.

I am also sensitive to energy and can feel The Divine working on me. My energy sensitivity occurred soon after my spiritual awakening. It is a divine gift continuing to evolve, and I cherish it. The Divine can also use the animal kingdom to deliver its messages.

I looked up the spiritual meanings of animals online not too long after my awakening process began. I often saw hawks perched above me, one after the other, on the sides of highways. They were each sitting on trees at the exact same height a quarter of a mile or so apart from each other.

This was not a coincidence because there are no coincidences. They were perched specifically to get my attention, which they always did and still do. When I see them, I tune into what they are wanting me to know. Usually, it is The Divine wanting me to see the higher perspective in a situation.

Hawks are usually perched up high in trees and have a bird's eye view, so it makes perfect sense to me The Divine would use a hawk to relay that type of message to me.

Magical whispers of insight,
Come ever so quickly,
In the silence of night.

Quick I am to jot them down,
So, they need not be lost,
And never found.

Stilling my mind before I go off to sleep.
In the morning, before arising,
They often do creep…

Into my thoughts so quick and sprite…
Oh, what glorious fun,
And utter delight.

Some of them profound, yes, that is true.
But some are everyday assistance,
That come on through.

"There's a package at the door," I often hear,
Or: "Wear your coat today,
It'll be cold my dear."

How so blessed we each truly are.
Always to be guided,
By our own shining star.

On one occasion, I showed up for my scheduled session with Divine Archangel Raphael and found a wonderful surprise. I was greeted at the front door. Kelly led me into the house and into her parlor where she conducted her sessions; however, her parlor was set up in a different way. I was surprised to see she had a massage table in the middle of the room.

"What's this for?" I asked.

She explained, "Well, last night, Archangel Raphael came and asked me to print out these pictures of the different Ascended Masters and archangels. Apparently, it's time for you to experience an initiation."

As I glanced down at the massage table, I noticed that pictures of the Ascended Masters, and the pictures of the three archangels were placed in specific locations. They were each placed in correlation with what would be my chakras.

Kelly instructed me to lie down on top of the pictures on the table, and then the initiation commenced.

Archangel Raphael, through Kelly, led the initiation ceremony by first making me aware this was a ceremony to open me up to channeling The Divine. These specific Ascended Masters and archangels were the ones I would be channeling. Archangel Raphael also informed me I would be channeling an additional four more Ascended Light Beings, but the angel did not provide me with their names.

There was light language spoken and there were two parts to the ceremony. The angel asked me how I would like to begin my channeling sessions.

Kelly Kolodney, the channeler of Divine Archangel Raphael, uses her singing voice to bring forth The Divine. She uses toning sounds that are some of the most beautiful angelic sounds I have ever heard.

I pondered for a moment, and then I told the angel I would like to use my speaking voice. I am a bit of a talker and thought it would be best, and Archangel Raphael smiled and agreed.

When the initiation ceremony concluded, Divine Archangel Raphael explained I would now be able to channel those specific divine light beings clearly.

I was excited, appreciative, and extremely thankful to The Divine for this beautiful gift. I was asked to practice often and to exercise this new gift I had received.

Oh, keeper of the light flame,
I love you so.
Buried deep within the mountain,
You did go.

Waiting ever so patiently,
You do,
Until a time,
When we see true…

The love within,
That holds us dear,
The one eternal heart,
That has no fear.

Oh, how grateful I am,
For when we meet,
Our reunion now upon us,
Will be ever so sweet.

TAKEAWAYS FOR YOUR TOOLBOX

In the beginning of my awakening journey, synchronistic messages from The Divine, and what I will call *transcendental experiences*, became almost regular occurrences for me. As always, there was a divine purpose at the root of all these experiences. It is my feeling The Divine was pulling out all the stops to catch and capture my attention. I was not aware of it at the time, but I feel it was very important then for me to *get on board quickly* with my divine soul's purpose and to place all my focus and attention there.

Although there is truly no *time*, as all exists in the eternal now, there is linear time we all collectively have agreed to take part in on this Earth plane, for the sake of the Earth experience. Looking back, I know now I had a window of opportunity placed before me, and it was for me to decide quickly if I was going to say yes to what was being offered.

Transcendental experiences and synchronistic events continuously occur in my life. However, these experiences are not as frequent as they were initially. I feel they don't need to be. I am aligned, attuned, and merged with my "I AM Presence" and flowing in a direction that is aligned with my soul's mission. I feel and know these amazing outer-worldly experiences arrived and did their job with absolute divine perfection and accomplished exactly what they set out to do. They gifted me with the remembrance of who it is I truly am, and I am forever grateful for that blessing.

Affirmations to Invite Divine
Synchronicity into Your Life

I AM intending, commanding, and demanding, I AM the *Victory* of inviting synchronicity to grace my life with ease, flow, and infinite abundance; so be it, and so it is.

I AM intending, commanding, and demanding, I AM the *Victory* of being in full alignment with my "I AM Presence" and I AM always fully supported, protected, and loved; so be it, and so it is.

I AM intending, commanding, and demanding, I AM the *Victory* of the oneness, the consciousness, and the pure knowing that everything comes to me in perfect divine time and order. The synchronicities I experience are a sign to let me know I AM aligned with my "I AM Presence" who lovingly guides me to my greatest possibilities of infinite potential; so be it, and so it is.

I AM intending, commanding, and demanding, I AM the *Victory* of the oneness and the consciousness and pure knowing that the synchronicities I experience in my life are a sign I AM in the flow; so be it, and so it is.

I AM intending, commanding, and demanding, I AM the *Victory* of the oneness and the consciousness and the pure knowing that I AM ever attuned to my soul's purpose and my entire life reflects this knowing; so be it, and so it is.

I AM intending, commanding, and demanding, I AM the *Victory* of the oneness, the consciousness, and the pure knowing that divine love brings me everything I need to grow, prosper, and experience in this moment; so be it, and so it is.

I AM intending, commanding, and demanding all is always in perfect divine time and order, and I AM always right where I AM meant to be at any given moment, now, continuously, and for all eternity itself sustained; so be it, and so it is.

I AM intending, commanding, and demanding as I open my heart to all that is good, I attract great and wonderful experiences to myself; so be it, and so it is.

Chapter Thirteen

The Quest

On August 4, 2014, my son and I embarked on what Archangel Raphael described to us as a divine, magical quest. The angel suggested to both my son and me that it would be advantageous for us to take a trip to Mount Shasta, California, which I knew absolutely nothing about prior to the angel mentioning it.

The mountain is a mystical power source for this planet. Many Ascended Light Beings are found there, and I was told by Archangel Raphael the Ascended Masters Flame is lit on the mountain. Mount Shasta is also the home of the present day Lemurians.

The Lemurians were the survivors of the sinking continent of Mu over 12,000 years ago. They are physically alive and well and living in the fifth-dimensional subterranean city of Telos located beneath Mount Shasta. It was prior to the sinking of their continent that the ancient Lemurians, fully aware of the destiny of their beloved continent, used their mastery of energy, crystals, sound, and vibrations, and carved out an inner city for themselves. It was their intention to preserve their culture, their treasures, and their records of ancient Earth's history.

It is said the large continent disappeared overnight into the Pacific Ocean over 12,000 years ago in a vast cataclysm. All the inhabitants of the Earth considered Lemuria, the land of Mu, their motherland, and there was a great upset when this event occurred.

Many Lemurians were able to migrate into the interior of Mount Shasta, which is said to have been one of the most important of their various administration centers prior to the sinking of their motherland.

These beautiful divine Ascended Light Beings, who are living in unity consciousness, are assisting humanity in many ways relating to our ascension.

Fields of flowers,
Abundantly grow,
In a special place,
I've come to know.

A place of crystalline,
Diamond light,
Where castles are majestically revealed,
In plain sight.

A place I often,
Choose to go,
To meet with those,
That love me so.

A warm greeting at first,
Then we walk hand in hand.
Perhaps this time,
To a magical land.

None of it matters,
Not really, that's for sure.
For together again,
We are once more.

In this special place,
That I have come to know,
Dear beloved light of the universe,
I love you so.

Archangel Raphael suggested both my son and I take the trip to Mount Shasta. The angel made sure we understood it wasn't a necessary trip; however, if we decided to take this trip, it would allow for a quickening of our ascension to occur. It would be an elevation of our vibrations.

Archangel Raphael explained once we placed ourselves in the airplane, we would be entering into a portal of divine alchemy and divine magic. We were also told we would remain in this magical portal for the entire length of our trip until we landed back in our hometown. It was explained by the angel, the period between the entry and exit points would be an opportunity for both my son and me to experience delicious magic. We would be connecting with others on the trip, and we would be reawakening and aligning with the essence of who it is we truly are.

Since the Ascended Masters' Flames are lit and amplified on the mountain, there is an ability to connect with them. This trip would also be a way for my son and me to reacquaint ourselves with the vibrations of these ascended dimensions and to connect to specific divine codes of light. Being present on the mountain would enable us to receive these downloads much easier than if we were at home.

Of course, my son and I were thrilled at the thought of going on a divine, magical adventure. After we had made our decision to go on the trip, Archangel Raphael described numerous places for us to visit during our stay in Mount Shasta. The angel gave us a to-do list for our visit. On the list were places we needed to connect into, as well as the names of different light beings we were meant to meet with.

We were off on one of the most magical adventures my son and I had ever had the opportunity to embark on. Neither of us had any idea what was to come and how magical it would truly be.

We were told by Archangel Raphael at the base of the mountain we would begin to feel its energy as we drove through, beginning our ascent and making our way up the mountain to its plateau. The angel went on further to explain we would begin to feel the welcoming of the pine trees as we ascended the mountain.

We were told that if we sat at sunset in meditation, we would receive greater divine light codes allowing us to connect with Ascended Beings of Light to assist humanity in its healing process.

Blessings from the stars,
Abound in this now.
Arriving in the heart of love,
Therefore, you allow.

Friends and family, from a distant time,
Now and before.
Oh, heavenly reunion,
Of that, you are sure.

Cherishing the visits,
And the magic they bring.
Allowing your heart to open wider,
Allowing your heart to sing.

For divine miraculous healings,
Can be upon you this day…
As you welcome your family of light,
Their infinite support here to stay.

We made the decision to travel during the month of August so all the trails we were asked by The Divine to visit would be open and available to us. When my son and I first arrived in Mount Shasta, we checked into our hotel and contacted a guide who we had made plans with before our journey began. Our guide was a woman who had lived there for many years. She was a divine channel and was happy to show us around a bit on our first day.

Our guide initially led us to a Lemurian portal on the mountain. My son, the guide, and I hiked to a spot on the mountain and sat down in the middle of a clearing. We were surrounded by some of the largest pine trees I have ever seen. We began our meditation which was a visit to the inner city of Telos, home of the Lemurians.

Our guide led the meditation, assisting my son and me in our entrance to Telos, the fifth-dimensional city of light.

My meditation was vivid. I was taken down an elevator to Telos where I was greeted by two Telosian men and one Telosian woman. During my meditation, upon my arrival in Telos, I found myself immediately on what seemed to be a conveyor belt. It was similar to the ones you find in the airport, so you do not have to walk a far distance.

On either side of the conveyor belt were many light beings waving and saying hello to me. I could feel their energy was one of absolute pure excitement, joy, and unconditional love. It was a grand reception, and I felt so honored for what I perceived to be such a warm greeting. I also remember there were many children in the crowd waving hello to me.

My Telosian guides and I arrived at what appeared to be a great temple. In this great temple, there was an extremely large pyramid crystal. My Telosian guides asked me to touch it and I did.

As soon as I touched it, it began to glow and change colors. It was a magnificent kaleidoscope of rainbow light.

My guides asked, "What are your favorite colors?"

"I like all of the colors," I said.

They nodded and agreed with me. They were also fond of all the colors.

They proceeded to ask, "Where would you like to go next? What would you like to see?"

I thought about it for a moment before responding. "I would love to see your homes and where you live. And I want to see your gardens!"

We left the temple and walked a while before arriving at what I assumed was a traditional Telosian dwelling. This home looked like a crystalline castle from the outside. We walked inside and the first thing I saw was a large crystal in the center of the home. It was shaped like a pyramid, and it was a beautiful pale pink color.

I was greeted by a child who entered the home. The child first hugged me and then hugged one of the adult guides who was with me.

After the tour of one of their homes, we rode beautiful large white horses to a garden where their food was grown.

The scenery was vivid and beautiful. I swam underwater for a while, playing with some of the Telosian children, and I was brought back to the elevator by my guides once I had finished the tour to be taken back to the surface.

After the meditation, my son, the guide, and I then drove to an area on the mountain where our guide told us many portals and vortices are known to exist.

There was an Archangel Portal, a Manifestation Portal, an Akashic Portal, and a Rejuvenation Portal there. We allowed ourselves to experience all these portals, and we received the divine gifts offered to us.

In this place, a beautiful white butterfly with little black spots approached us and flew around my son, me, and our guide. The butterfly took a moment to land on each of us as if to say hello.

I felt called to a large clearing deep in the forest. I followed my intuitive guidance and went up a slight incline to a clearing. It was there I saw a large boulder lying on the forest floor, and it was then I heard the name, *Merlin's Egg.*

My son and I lay on top of the giant boulder, and as soon as we did, a short-statured light being came to the left side of us, and then it came to the right side of us. Its energy was palpable.

We were receiving an initiation as we lay on that boulder, and I could feel energetic work being done on my root chakra.

My son and I decided to part ways with our guide after thanking her, and we began to make our way to an area on the mountain known as Panther Creek. We found ourselves first on Grey Butte Trail. We took our time meandering through the meadow and then walked deeper into the forest.

There were many trees and boulders, and my son and I weren't certain if we were connecting to the specific boulders we were meant to be connecting with at that time.

It was at this point in our journey—because the mountain was so vast and there were so many locations to visit—that my son and I decided we needed another mountain guide. We needed someone who really knew the area well. I felt it would also be helpful to have a guide who would be open to understanding the spiritual significance of our trip.

I thought, if we could connect with a guide with those attributes, it would make finding and connecting to those places and specific beings of light who we were meant to connect with much easier.

I found I was second-guessing myself a bit and being concerned with checking things off my to-do list instead of going with the flow. However, by the third day, I had become more centered in my heart space, and I was allowing myself to listen, hear, and follow the guidance of my "I AM Presence."

The next thing we were meant to discover was a large boulder that looked like a chair.

"One could sit upon it," the angel said.

Archangel Raphael explained it was a chair that Ascended Light Beings sat down upon. When the Ascended Light Beings sit upon this chair, other light beings are lined up in a single file coming down from the top of the mountain to receive divine blessings and teachings.

Near this Ascended Masters' chair, there would be another rock formation we were meant to find and connect with as well. This rock formation, as the angel described, would be in the shape of a heart. The angel said there would be no mistaking it whatsoever. Also, there would be a third rock formation in the form of an infinity symbol.

The angel then explained these three rock formations create the formation of a triangle. This triangle is a portal opening of what one would think of as the Merkaba. We were told as we stand within this triangle—this portal—the energies would be strong and powerful. We were told there would be light beings, who would approach us, and would be friendly with us.

It was told to us that these Ascended Light Beings would have specific messages for us, and we would be able to communicate with them directly while we were on the mountain.

Almost immediately, my son and I found what clearly appeared to be a heart-shaped rock formation. We quickly glanced around the area to look for the other formations we were meant to connect with before heading further up the mountain, which was extremely steep.

Mount Shasta is breathtaking and mesmerizing which seemed to help take our attention off the blazing temperatures. Regardless, we were both so happy and grateful to be in Mount Shasta and experiencing something utterly amazing.

We decided to continue our trek up the mountain, heading this time toward the mountain's left side. After approximately three hundred steps or so, we reached a small plateau that led to the backside of the mountain.

Intuitively, I was getting a strong indication we were headed the wrong way. My feeling was correct because as we walked on, still heading in the wrong direction, I fell. Or, should I say, I was stopped.

It was only a small scrape on my knee, but I received the message loud and clear from The Divine, and we decided to go back down the mountain, heading back toward our vehicle. Once back, my son and I found a rock that looked similar to a chair the angel had described to us. It was located quite a distance from the heart rock formation we had discovered almost immediately upon our arrival at the base plateau.

By this time, we had located two of the three formations we were meant to find. However, it was getting a bit late, and we were tired, so we made the decision to head back to the hotel.

We decided to go out for dinner that evening. It was there we met our waitress, Canbera. We shared our mission and told her we were in search of a mountain guide to assist us. Canbera was so sweet, and she told us she had a friend who lived on the mountain most of the time. This woman's name was Bonnie.

Canbera said she would give her friend a call and this woman, Bonnie, would more than likely be able to escort us up the mountain the next day.

We were beyond grateful and thrilled. I knew it was by no coincidence we *happened* to go to a restaurant that had a lovely waitress who *happened* to have a friend who lived on the mountain who would more than likely be able to escort us around. This is what is known as synchronicity at its best.

I thanked Canbera and told her I would give her friend a call at nine o'clock in the morning the next day.

The next morning, Bonnie did not answer on my first attempt to call her, so I left her a voice message. She quickly returned my call and drove to our hotel to meet with us. We introduced ourselves to her and had a chat before embarking on our day. She asked if she could listen to our recording from Divine Archangel Raphael, and we, of course, said yes.

After having listened to the recording, Bonnie was almost as excited as we were to be on and a part of this magical quest.

We explained to Bonnie we weren't sure if we had connected to the large boulders that we were meant to connect with on the day prior. She drove us straight back to Panther Creek, to the general area we had been the day before. This time, however, we walked up a different path. It is there we came upon some large boulders. These boulders were much larger than the ones my son and I had found the day prior. We then spent a good amount of time connecting to them and being sure to place our hands upon all of them. We then made our way back down to Bonnie's car, and she drove us up to the very top of the mountain.

We all got out of the car and walked up to the plateau, the place where the rock formations we were asked to find were located. I proceeded to show Bonnie the heart-shaped rock as well as the Ascended Masters' chair my son and I had located the day before. We then began to search for one remaining rock formation which was the infinity symbol, which seemed to be cleverly eluding us.

We had a good look around for some time and then decided to head back to Bonnie's car to get our lunches. As we were all gathered by Bonnie's car having a discussion, I heard a man's voice yelling at us from a distance.

He yelled over at us, "Hey, do you guys want to see the heart of the mountain?"

We looked at each other, and Bonnie whispered she thought we were meant to speak with him. We all unanimously replied, "Yes, we do."

With that, the man made his way over to us. He then showed us something that appeared to look like an aorta carved into the mountain. He also showed us Mother Mary carved into the mountain, which he told us was a natural carving and not man made.

I could not believe I had missed it, it seemed so obvious once he had pointed out the carving of Mother Mary. The mysterious man almost immediately asked us if we believed in spacecrafts.

We, once again, replied a unanimous yes.

He began speaking to us in an esoteric way where he was concentrating on and speaking and looking intently at my son. He began to speak of things that were otherworldly with such ease and with what seemed to be a pure knowing and an infinite wisdom.

He explained that the spacecrafts spiral through a wormhole and then they go down into the mountain. He spoke about the infinity symbol and how the spacecraft can land themselves on whatever electron they want, and then they can travel wherever they are wanting to go within the universe. He then formally introduced himself as Jacob and he told us he was a physicist.

He had long reddish hair, and he was wearing shorts. He asked if he could hug us almost immediately. I looked down at his shoes, which were sneakers with green wings on the tops of them. He told us he had made them himself and he picked up one of the wings of his sneaker and he showed us it was green underneath the wing as well.

As we were speaking, a woman seemed to appear out of nowhere and joined our gathering. She was clearly with Jacob, as he introduced her as his friend, but she never spoke a word. She was Asian and was wearing a unicorn hat, and when she turned around, I saw she had giant angel wings painted onto the back of her shirt.

We explained our quest to Jacob and shared that we were specifically looking for a rock formation in the form of an infinity symbol. He immediately said to follow him; he knew the vicinity of where it was.

Just then, my son and I watched in utter amazement as Jacob made his way up the mountain quickly, almost too quickly. He climbed the rocks like a mountain goat would, with great skill, precision, and speed.

My son turned to me with a look of both shock and excitement on his face. My son, Bonnie, and I all proceeded to follow our new friend Jacob back up the mountain, but at a much slower pace.

By this point, I was so curious as to who this man truly was, not to mention his friend who still hadn't uttered a single word since we had met her. On our way up the mountain, we stopped at a large rock and took a breather, and it was then my son wandered out of my sight.

I knew he was only steps away from me, but part of the mountain was blocking my view. When he did wander off, I watched as Jacob and the mysterious woman followed along behind him.

Bonnie spoke to me and said she felt everything was all right. My son was only out of my sight for five minutes, but as a mother, it made me a bit nervous.

When I went to retrieve my son, I found them all in deep discussion. My son came back to our resting spot with me, and Jacob and his friend followed us and asked us if we wanted to chant Om with them. We decided not to as we were about to eat lunch; however, looking back, I wish we had taken the time to chant with them, but all is always in divine time and order and this experience unfolded with perfection.

Jacob then told us he and his friend were going to make their way up to the top of the mountain. We all said our goodbyes to each other as we watched Jacob and his female friend hike up the mountain and disappear into the distance.

My son, Bonnie, and I ate our lunch on the mountain amongst some rather friendly chipmunks. Afterward, we decided to go to a place called Ascension Rock. This had not been on our to-do list from the angel; however, Bonnie explained it was of great significance. The rock formation was humongous. It is said the Lemurian Council of Twelve resides under the rock formation.

After our quick visit to Ascension Rock, we made our way back down to the foot of the mountain to a place called City Park.

The Sacramento Headwaters, which is right in Mount Shasta City Park, is the birthing place of the Sacramento River. Its water is said to be pristine and pure, and it is said to hold great healing powers. It is world-renowned and many locals head to this spot with their large, empty bottles to fill. It is also said drinking these waters is a wonderful way to purify, cleanse, and align yourself. The water is known by many to be pure magic.

We arrived at City Park, and we went straight to the water source. There were many people wading in the water and wetting their hair and collecting drinking water from the spring. I had an empty water bottle, as did my son, so we filled up our bottles and began to drink the healing waters.

Just as we were leaving, making our way to Bonnie's car, Jacob and his female friend pulled up in a car behind us and parked. They proceeded to get out of their car, and they walked straight toward us. It was odd because the last time we had seen them they were both supposedly making their way further up the mountain.

We had not been at City Park for long and it takes a good twenty or so minutes to drive back down to the bottom of the mountain. This struck me as strange almost immediately.

Jacob and his female friend asked us if we had a chance to drink the water.

I replied yes. I told Jacob we had each filled up our bottles and had tasted the water. Jacob seemed pleased with that response and then he walked into the water and wet his hair. We said our goodbyes once again and then Bonnie dropped both my son and me off at our hotel.

It wasn't until we returned from our trip, we discovered how much magic had truly occurred. Archangel Raphael told my son and me after we had returned, that Jacob was not human, he was not from Earth.

It was only then I really remembered what the angel had told us before we even left for our trip. Archangel Raphael had told us upon touching the boulders we would gain access to the Ascended Masters in a truly magical way. It would be a way in which the Ascended Masters could manifest at will into form, and they could speak to us. Archangel Raphael explained that by touching us, they would be able to open our DNA.

I then recalled Jacob hugging both my son and me when we had first met. I also remembered the strange outfits they both were wearing, which, looking back, were hints they were not from this dimension.

Archangel Raphael told us when we had the experience of meeting the Ascended Masters, we would begin to question whether they were from Earth or not as we spoke to them. That is exactly what occurred.

Jacob, and especially the Asian woman who never spoke a word, had ethereal qualities about them. I feel we were speaking and communicating with Ascended Master Hilarion and Ascended Master Kuan Yin.

Mother Mary can come in many forms, as we were reminded by Archangel Raphael before our trip, one of which is the Ascended Master Kuan Yin. She is the goddess of compassion and Hilarion is the Cohan of The Fifth Ray of Healing and Truth.

My son has always had a special connection to Ascended Master Hilarion, and Jacob's green-winged shoes and telling us he was a physicist were huge hints. Ascended Master Hilarion emits a green ray of light, like the green on his shoes.

My son and I received all we were meant to receive. I know this because, once again, all is always in divine time and order and there is absolutely no such thing as happenstance.

TAKEAWAYS FOR YOUR TOOLBOX

This trip awakened me to the remembering that when we allow ourselves to release old belief systems and ways of being that no longer serve us, pure magic then has space to arise. I had several years of experience of being on my soul's journey, which allowed me to be in the exact space I felt I needed to be in to fully immerse myself in this adventure. If someone had said to me several years prior that I would be sent on a magical quest by an angel to awaken my DNA in order to raise my consciousness, and I would meet beings of light who can instantaneously come into forms that I would converse with, I would have said they were crazy.

It all begins with loving yourself and all others as self. When you allow yourself to do this and be this, you begin to see glimpses of what you may feel as miraculous. However, where it is we truly come from, miracles are the way of it.

Affirmations to Assist in Opening to the
Divine Magic Within

I AM commanding, demanding, and intending, I AM the *Victory* of allowing myself to see with eyes of innocent perception; so be it, and so it is.

I AM commanding, demanding, and intending, I AM the *Victory* of being divine and divine perfection, now and for all eternity itself sustained; so be it, and so it is.

I AM commanding, demanding, and intending, I AM the *Victory* of releasing to the light all incoherent energies, limiting belief systems, shadow thoughts from my thinking mind, and discordant energies from my feeling world that no longer serve my highest good; so be it, and so it is.

I AM commanding, demanding, and intending, I AM the *Victory* of the oneness, the consciousness, and the pure knowing. There is nothing I have to have, do, or be, other than what I am being right now, which is always enough; so be it, and so it is.

I AM commanding, demanding, and intending, I AM the *Victory* of loving myself unconditionally beyond measure, more than anything, as the divine perfection I always am; so be it, and so it is.

I AM commanding, demanding, and intending, I AM the *Victory* of always being one with and always experiencing a joyful, healthy, abundant, peaceful, free, harmonious life, now and for all eternity itself sustained; so be it, and so it is.

Chapter Fourteen

Gratitude

*T*he next spring, my son and I decided again to go see the Philadelphia Phillies during their spring training in Clearwater Beach, Florida. This time, I decided to meet an old friend whose son was the same age as mine.

Upon returning home from my trip, I noticed my favorite manicure scissors were missing. It seemed I had misplaced my sunglasses as well. I had a strong, intuitive feeling I had left my sunglasses in Florida, but I could not remember the last time I had seen my manicure scissors. I always kept them in my makeup case, and they weren't there when I went to look for them. I ended up turning my apartment upside down searching for them.

During the search for my manicure scissors, a thought entered my awareness. I remembered reading on an oracle card The Divine, specifically Archangel Chamuel, can help find lost things. The angel is also known to assist one in finding their purpose.

I was certainly needing help finding my scissors that day, and I decided to ask Archangel Chamuel for assistance in finding them.

Breathe in the sweetness of life,
Pure joy, the angels say,
Find something to really appreciate,
This glorious, beautiful day.

It can be as simple as being grateful,
For just one breath taken in,
And with this, dear one,
You truly can begin.

For the magical gift of abundance,
Is truly knowing your worth,
Being thankful for what you already have,
Right here on Mother Earth.

For we are the Master Creators,
We choose what will be,
And focusing on what you desire,
Brings more of the same you see.

Your thoughts are an order,
Placed continuously to the universe within,
Which tells that universe,
Just what experience you'd like to begin.

Later, I walked outside of my apartment to sweep the breezeway near my front door and clean off my doormat. It was a windy day and some leaves had gathered there.

I went to the kitchen closet, found the broom, and opened the front door of my apartment. I then stepped outside and lifted my front doormat. I could not believe what I was seeing.

Under my doormat, on top of a rectangular-shaped bed of the whitest sand I have ever seen, were my manicure scissors. They were centered perfectly *underneath* my doormat. The closest beach to my apartment was located on the Jersey Shore, but I can tell you I have never seen sand that white from New Jersey. This was most definitely Clearwater Beach sand.

I knew the moment I had discovered my manicure scissors under my front doormat that I had left them in Florida. The Divine had returned them to me.

I was amazed, once again. It was as if they were being presented to me as a gift, and in fact, they truly were. The sand was carved out into the shape of a perfect rectangle. The bed of sand the scissors were lying on was approximately three inches in length and about an inch thick.

I also recall the name *Archangel Metatron* coming into my awareness the moment I discovered the manicure scissors.

I felt it was that archangel who had returned the scissors to me. It truly was a divine, magical experience I will never forget. I thanked The Divine that day, expressing my deepest appreciation and gratitude for the magnificent gift of my scissors being returned.

The Divine is always speaking to us, helping us each remember who it is we are. The Divine is always letting us know, through our experiences, the realm of the miraculous is the norm, and not the other way around. The Divine was helping me to remember, through this experience, there is absolutely nothing that cannot be done through and with our Creative Source. Also, there is nothing that cannot be done through and with each of us because we are one with our Creator.

I have found these divine messages and experiences have many different meanings for us when they occur. I feel being present to receive these divine gifts, and being grateful for them when they occur, are the keys to unwrapping the divine gift given in its full glory.

Concrete, solid,
So real, it seems to be.
Oh, but that's the pure magic
Of it all, believe you, me.

Designed to be that way,
By the Creator of the All.
No task impossible,
No task difficult, grand or small.

All potentials,
They are you see…
Not one, not some,
But all can be.

A solution from nowhere,
And everywhere… It arrives.
Bringing miracles,
To the most desperate of lives.

Never ever believe,
That all is lost.
That is the illusion,
And it has a cost.

Believe in the great mystery,
Divine magic, and all that can be.
Believe in solutions,
Your eyes cannot yet see.

For out of the ethers,
That which you wish for will appear.
No need to seek it,
It is already here.

TAKEAWAYS FOR YOUR TOOLBOX

The eternal now is the only time that exists. The past is history, the future is a mystery, and the gift is in the present. The more you can bring your awareness back into the now—the present moment—the more you are able to fully live and receive all the gifts life has for you.

Time is truly an illusion; it is something we, as a collective humanity, created, which enables us to move through this Earth's reality. Returning to your breath is a wonderful way to bring your awareness back to the present. When you are in the now, in acceptance of what is, you can enjoy the fullness of your entire experience in each moment with gratitude. You are then one with the universal flow, which places you in the receptive mode for magnificent divine blessings.

When you are actively grateful, you receive more to be grateful for.

Affirmations to Assist You in Being
Present and in the Receptive Mode

I AM commanding, demanding, and intending, I AM the *Victory* of choosing to always be one with my "I AM Presence," the fullness of all I have become, my highest timeline, and my highest resonance and light; so be it, and so it is.

I AM commanding, demanding, and intending, I AM the *Victory* of choosing to always be in full acceptance of myself, of what is, and I AM always choosing to be eager for more; so be it, and so it is.

I AM commanding, demanding, and intending, I AM the *Victory* of choosing to always be in the receptive mode for all I desire, that serves my highest good, and the highest good of all, and is always aligned with divine will; so be it, and so it is.

I AM commanding, demanding, and intending, I AM the *Victory* of the oneness, the consciousness, and the pure knowing that the more I express my gratitude, the more I receive more to be grateful for; so be it, and so it is.

I AM commanding, demanding, and intending, I AM the *Victory* of being so grateful that "I AM That I AM," now and for all eternity itself sustained; so be it, and so it is.

I AM commanding, demanding, and intending, I AM the *Victory* of being so grateful for all the infinite, divine blessings in my life, both big and small; so be it, and so it is.

I AM commanding, demanding, and intending, I AM the *Victory* of having everything always work out for my best-case scenario, now, continuously, and for all eternity itself sustained; so be it, and so it is.

I AM commanding, demanding, and intending, I AM the *Victory* of being one with and always centered in my open, pure, grateful, appreciative heart, which is always ever expanding, and which I AM anchored and centered in, at any given moment, now, continuously, and for all eternity itself sustained; so be it, and so it is.

Chapter Fifteen

Service

*I*t was an exciting time and a brand-new opportunity presented to me. It was an opportunity that enabled me the chance to serve in co-creation with The Divine, along with a group of others, to bring forth healing for humanity and for Mother Earth.

Archangel Raphael, through the channeler, Kelly Kolodney, offered a group class, Birthing Your Angelic Self. Its purpose was to encourage those in the group to embody their angelic selves, their "I AM Presence."

Each member of the group, through their own free will, worked right alongside The Divine to serve the light. One of our projects involved our entire group splitting into groups of four or five people each. Each member of the group was assigned to work with an Ascended Master or an Archangel, who were all members of The Council of Light.

The Council of Light is a group of Ascended Beings of Light. They are a team of Ascended Masters, light beings, angels, and divine guides devoted to the rising of Earth and all of humanity into higher states of consciousness. It is from them you receive your personal mission. They are similar to the United Nations of the spirit world.

You can call upon them for help and assistance at any time regarding your personal mission.

We visited The Council of Light during our group meditation led by Archangel Raphael. In our etheric bodies, each group member picked a seat around a large table where the Ascended Light Beings were already seated. After being seated, we were then given instructions to look to our left, for the Light Being who would become our mentor.

As I turned, I saw Jesus sitting right next to me. I also remember Mother Mary was directly across the table from me, and to my right Lord Melchizedek was seated.

I had a strong feeling my mentor was going to be Yeshua. I am a healer, and I had been connecting more and more to this Master's energy throughout my ascension process. I felt it was a perfect divine match and I was thrilled.

After we were assigned our mentors, we split up into our groups. We were each given a specific project assigned to us by Archangel Raphael.

My group was assigned to The Ganges River. We were then paired up with several Ascended Light Beings and members of the angelic realm to work together on healing the river and all those who bathed in it.

The Ganges, or Ganga as it is sometimes known, is a river of South Asia which flows through India and Bangladesh. The river is a lifeline to millions who live along its course. It is also known to be a sacred river and worshipped as the goddess Ganga in Hinduism.

It was told to our group that the river was toxic. Many people were bathing in it while garbage and trash were being thrown into the river daily. It was our service work to join with the Ascended Beings of Light to purify, bless, and transmute the water in The Ganges, returning it to its pure state.

All the members of our group were meeting The Divine halfway and asking and intending for them to assist during our time of service. It was a group effort, and it needed both sides to participate for it to manifest in the way we were all intending. This is how the universe works. It is a co-creation; we are never alone, and we are never manifesting by ourselves.

I, along with the members of my group who were working on The Ganges River project, worked directly with John the Baptist, who works with blessing and purifying those who drop into the waters to be anointed and blessed. Therefore, it made perfect sense he would be one of the Ascended Light Beings assigned to assist our group.

We worked as a team in the cleansing and purifying of the waters and the people who were bathing in them. Using our light body Merkabas during meditation, we traveled to The Ganges River. Once we arrived, we invited the Ascended Masters' energy to join us, as we dropped down in our light body Merkabas into the river. Once in the river, underneath the water with our energy merged with the Ascended Masters' energy, we began to purify and transmute the water.

Merkaba is a word that comes from Hebrew, and it translates to "chariot" or "thing to ride in." It is a vehicle the etheric body uses to travel in to access higher states of consciousness. "Mer" means divine light. "Ka" represents your spirit, and "Ba" is your body. It is when you combine the strength of the light, the spirit, and the body, you can reach a completely balanced and harmonious level that helps you channel your energy to connect to the higher consciousness. This is the mode of transportation we—all of us doing this service work—were utilizing to travel to these specific places to do this most sacred work.

We felt and knew the beauty and the sacredness of the river. We began to see those positive aspects of the river moving into the cells of those who were bathing in it. We intended all those in the water of The Ganges River were receiving healing and love. We did all this through meditation each day.

There was also a second part to our sacred work. The Divine had asked each of us to acquire a glass jar. We were then asked to write the title of the specific project we were working on and place that title on the jar.

I wrote Ganges River on a piece of paper and taped it to the side of my jar. I also taped a map I had found online of The Ganges River to the jar. Next, we were asked by the Ascended Masters to fill the jar with water. This water was to symbolize and represent the water of The Ganges River—or whatever project we were assigned to.

The Ascended Masters asked us to hold the jar of water in our hands while we meditated each day. All the members of our group then meditated on visualizing the water being totally transmuted, and all the garbage in the water being released. We were also asked to intend and see the water of The Ganges coming back to life, purified, and filled with love. This would allow oxygen to move through the water once again.

We also blessed the sacredness of all the water of The Ganges, seeing its beauty and its purified state moving back into the cells of all those bathing in it, allowing all the bathers to receive healing and love.

This was one example of the type of service we were co-creating with The Divine as a group.

I once read The Creative Source of All That Is, *God,* is always in service to all. We are each an extension of Source Energy. Therefore, to be more in alignment with who it is we truly are, we can choose to be in service to all. When we serve others, through our open, pure, grateful, appreciative hearts, we are truly serving ourselves at the same time because we are one. There is no greater gift.

As you gather together to serve others,
The angels begin to sing.
As you gather together to serve others,
A bell in Heaven, it does ring.

As you gather together to serve others,
Blessings begin to fall,
Not just upon those you serve,
But, for everyone and all.

As you gather together to serve others,
The Great Masters then join in,
And amplify with your heart's intent,
Infinite blessings then begin.

As you gather together to serve others,
The universe then serves you.
For the one you all gather to serve,
Is the one and only you.

It was during my years in sessions with Simona I began to try my hand at painting. Until this point in my life, I had never really thought of myself as an artist. I thought of myself as more of a poet. I loved writing poems, and when I was seventeen, I wrote a children's short story all in rhyme.

It was during a channeled session with Simona The Divine spoke through her and asked me if I recalled drawing pictures as a child.

At first, I answered no. Other than drawing pictures in school as a young child, along with the other children, I had no memory whatsoever of being an avid illustrator. It was then that The Divine brought forth a memory.

I saw myself drawing all sorts of characters, houses, trees, and other things. It was during this period I was also receiving information from The Divine, through my own intuition, to begin to channel divine art. I was feeling a powerful urge to begin to paint.

I researched the different mediums used in painting, and I chose acrylics. I had no idea what I was doing; however, I had followed several amazing artists on social media and learned the initial process of how to begin. I gathered my supplies and created a small art studio on the first floor of my home.

I was excited to begin. I loved the variety of colors of the paints, and I approached it as a new adventure. As I began to paint for the first time, I noticed I was painting similar images repeatedly. I was painting what appeared to be spirals.

I made it a point to surrender absolutely everything and all to The Divine each day and whenever it happened to come into my awareness to do so. I knew even though this was a different way of expressing myself, through painting instead of writing, the divine love and the divine messages were still flowing through me and to me onto my canvas.

The Divine explained these light spirals carried and were infused with divine light codes which awakened the remembrance of All That Is for those who encountered them through my art. They also, being divinely light encoded, awakened one's soul mission by a mere glance upon them. I painted these spirals in many different shapes, sizes, and colors.

After I had been painting for a year or so, it was time for me to put my light spiral paintings on display. I decided to enter several expositions that enabled my art to be displayed to the public.

Simona painted angels, whales, and all sorts of beautiful divine beings of light, so we decided to have our booths positioned next to each other during one of the expositions we attended. During this exposition, we both had scheduled presentations to give as well.

My discussion about oneness was scheduled in a time slot before Simona's presentation. It was a Saturday, and it had been raining for almost two weeks straight. However, on that day, we had our first sunny day in a long time.

We did not have many people passing by our booths that day. We knew everyone was outside enjoying the first sunshine they had seen in a long while, and we couldn't blame them.

My cousin and my best friend were also with us on the day of the exposition. They came as a favor to us, assisting us with the selling of our art, and they also helped take care of our booths when Simona and I had to leave and give our individual presentations.

Simona and I both questioned whether we should return to the expo the next day because the expo did not seem to be attracting many patrons. Since it wasn't busy, we all sat in a circle and began talking with each other and sharing our spiritually related stories.

Simona began to share some transcendental experiences she had gone through along her journey. She explained she remembered a time when someone she did not know approached her and spoke to her. She explained it felt like an odd conversation.

Simona always had magical, mystical tales to tell, and when she spoke, all were attentive and hanging on every word. Simona explained when the person who she had conversed with walked away from her, she had an intuitive feeling she had spoken to Mother Mary. This indeed was a special, transcendental encounter.

When it came time for me to give my presentation at the expo, it was around two o'clock in the afternoon. I went into the presentation room and saw I had an audience of approximately fifteen people. In all honesty, I was surprised to even have that many people show up to my presentation. The number of patrons at the expo seemed to be dwindling as the day progressed.

After my presentation concluded, I returned to my booth, and I began talking again with my best friend and my cousin. I also conducted an occasional oracle card reading for patrons who were wanting one. Whenever someone approached either my table or Simona's table, where our artwork was on display, my friend and my cousin would answer any questions the potential customers had.

Around four o'clock in the afternoon, while Simona was still giving her presentation, an elderly gentleman approached Simona's table and then quickly made his way to my table. He stood directly in front of me.

My cousin and my best friend were involved in a deep conversation, and I was not giving a reading to anyone, so I stood up to greet the man. I began to explain to the elderly gentleman exactly what my light spiral paintings were about and the divine qualities they possessed. I also pointed out and showed the gentleman some paintings I had recently completed.

I told him my painting was evolving, it was moving from solely painting light spirals to trying my hand at painting other subjects, as well.

It was in that moment, before the elderly man even uttered a word, I felt a powerful energy begin to swirl and move within me, around me, and through me. I was standing feet away from the elderly gentleman and I was then amid what felt like a sea of energy.

He spoke to me, looking straight into my eyes. The gentleman said he was so happy I was evolving; he would be concerned if I wasn't. He then looked deep into my eyes and said, "I am also happy you are here."

I then heard and felt the name *Jesus* come over me. Our eyes were locked, and I was still feeling powerful love energy enfolding me and within me. It was then I saw a twinkle of light in his eyes. He kept repeating his name over and over to me telepathically.

While this was occurring, I could hear my best friend and cousin speaking in the background, almost like a muffled, muted sound. They were oblivious to what was going on, still deep in their own conversation.

I answered Jesus back telepathically. I told him, as he was repeating his name to me, I knew who he was. I kept saying, "I know it's you. I know it's you."

The elderly gentleman smiled and then turned and began to walk away. The feeling of the swirling bubble of energy that had been surrounding me two seconds prior was gone in an instant.

I turned to my best friend and my cousin with a look of utter amazement on my face and began to explain to them what had occurred. Into my awareness quickly flooded the recollection of Simona sharing her own experience of the time she felt like she had been speaking to Mother Mary through another person.

I knew, at that moment, Simona had told me that story earlier because Jesus was about to make an appearance in the afternoon. Everything connected for me in that one moment.

Just as I had that epiphany, Simona came walking around the corner, having finished her presentation.

With utter excitement, I ran to her side and began to tell her the story of what I had experienced.

Simona, after hearing what had occurred, had a blank stare while she took a moment to tune into her spirit guides, asking them what had taken place. She smiled and nodded her head saying yes, it was him. I told her I knew it was him and he delivered, not only to me but to both of us, an important message to stay put at the expo, and to show up the following day.

Of course, The Divine, of which we are all always one with, had heard Simona and me contemplating not coming in the next day due to low patron attendance at the expo.

Simona laughed and said yes, she was returning on Sunday, and I said I would also attend the expo the next day. The following day, the exposition had a much larger number of people in attendance, and both Simona and I were glad we had decided to be present.

That experience really helped me to remember, as awakened beings of light, we really have so much to offer. Even if it is for one person who may need help, that's always enough of a reason to be present and supportive.

I know all things are possible through and with The Divine. The Divine can easily manifest in any form they choose at any given moment. The Divine can also enter a person's consciousness and speak through them. This is exactly the scenario I feel occurred for me on that Saturday at the expo.

The elderly gentleman, who Jesus channeled his message through, happened to be helping his son attend a booth for the weekend. I saw the elderly gentleman the next day, as he passed by my booth once again with a smile on his face.

This encounter with Jesus was a wonderful surprise and a beautiful experience I will remember and treasure always.

As we each love ourselves and all others as ourselves, we can then open to infinite possibilities. The universe shows us these infinite possibilities through our own experiences, which then begin to reveal themselves to us. What follows and then begins to develop and solidify within is such a profound, clear, pure knowing and a strong foundation. It is a foundation that cannot be toppled, and it is based in the truth of who it is you truly are.

See me everywhere,
And within everything.
There is no one else here,
May that truth within ring.

For as you treat yourself as,
And with the very best…
You allow that for all others,
You allow it for the rest.

You are the universe.
It all lies in you.
And as you do for self,
You do for others too.

For loving self,
Is always loving me.
There is absolutely no separation,
None at all you see.

I AM the Creator of Worlds,
And so are you.
I know I AM worthy,
Do you think you are worthy too?

Know who you are now,
That we are one and the same.
We are the Creative Source,
And that is our name.

I love you forevermore.

As I mentioned previously, I recalled writing a story in rhyme when I was a teenager. It was during this part of my journey The Divine asked me to do my best to locate that story.

I had no idea where it could be. We had moved residences so many times when I was young, and I had no clue as to where to even begin looking for the manuscript.

Finally, it dawned on me that I had stuck it in a book for safekeeping. I had no idea as to what specific book or what specific residence it was in.

I went to my parents' house and searched for it in their library to no avail. Since I could not seem to find the manuscript anywhere, I decided to sit down and do my best to recreate the story from my own memory.

To my surprise, as I began to write, and as I allowed myself to surrender to the process, the entire story flowed back with pure divine clarity. I looked up at the clock and realized I had finished writing the entire manuscript in only one hour's time.

I felt the words on the page had come directly from my soul, and it felt as though they had literally poured right out of me.

To be honest, I don't even recall much of the writing process. I was dumbfounded at the short amount of time it took to recreate.

It was a children's story, and three more stories were soon to follow.

I read all my children's stories to Simona one day over the phone. She began to cry as I was reading them to her, and she told me how much these stories of unity and oneness were needed right now within humanity. She told me she felt these divinely channeled stories were meant for not just children to hear, but for all ages.

As we each remember we are love at our true essence and we begin to love ourselves and all others as self, a whole new world opens up to each of us. It is a New Earth only perceived by your open, pure heart.

The New Earth is here now, and it is available at any given moment for you. The choice given in each moment is to align and to choose to be the love you are. This always begins with love of self, first and foremost, and love of all *as* self. It is always an opportunity to choose love over fear in each moment. It is an asking of *What would be the most loving thing I could do for myself right now?* from your absolute highest perspective, and then following that guidance throughout every aspect of your life.

A magical poem,
Of enchantment and delight,
I now sit down,
And begin to write.

Never knowing the healing messages,
That she will bring,
Or what on this night,
Will make her heart sing.

I only trust,
As she guides me along...
Each twist and turn,
A melody of song.

A mutual trust,
Has grown this way.
I don't need to know,
What she has to say.

She gives me an inkling,
That's enough for me.
What follows is always...
We shall see.

I trust her completely,
With pen in hand.
For this is the way of it,
I now understand.

TAKEAWAYS FOR YOUR TOOLBOX

The Creative Source of All That Is is always in service for the highest good of all. This is what I was remembering as my service work with The Divine commenced. When you serve your fellow man and all of creation with kindness, compassion, and a pure heart, you are serving yourself. This is because there is only one here in truth.

It is important to mention this service is best offered with pure intention, through pure unconditional love, and with a true desire to serve with compassion. As more of us begin to wake up and realize we are one with all things, compassion for all others and all of creation itself can emerge through love. When you know you are absolutely one with the person that you may see on the street in need, you are more likely to help rather than pass by.

Affirmations to Support You in Your
Service to the Light

I AM commanding, demanding, and intending, I AM the *Victory* of serving the light that serves me, while always one with and experiencing divine perfect health and well-being, infinite joy, bliss and happiness, infinite abundance, divine eternal peace, divine perfect balance, and harmony; so be it, and so it is.

I AM commanding, demanding, and intending, dear benevolent Source of All That Is, please make me a channel for divine creativity and an instrument of a higher will, always for my highest good and for the highest good of all; so be it, and so it is.

I AM commanding, demanding, and intending, I AM the *Victory* of being God Source Consciousness, I live for the world, and I choose to be now; so be it, and so it is.

I AM commanding, demanding, and intending, dear Creative Source of All That Is, please divinely bless me now and always with all I need, all I need to know, and joy or better at any given moment, now, continuously and for all eternity itself sustained, and may it be aligned always with divine will, for my highest good and for the highest good of all; so be it, and so it is.

I AM commanding, demanding, and intending, I AM the *Victory* of choosing to be divinely guided by the light of the universe that dwells within me, for my highest good, and for the highest good of all, now and for all eternity itself sustained; so be it, and so it is.

Chapter Sixteen

The Divine Plan Fulfilled

*T*he fulfillment of the divine plan is your eternal freedom. It is your homecoming to the wholeness you have always been. It is a remembering of who it is you truly are, along with the full embodiment of that truth.

You are one with all of creation and existence, and as such, you are omnipresent. You are one with all things as all things are one with you. The fulfillment of the divine plan is the awakening of your true self with an absolute knowing you are one with your "I AM Presence"; you are God itself. It is also the awakening to the truth that all of creation and existence, which you are one with, is also God, and it is all you.

We are each ever fulfilling the divine plan as it is an eternal one. For time immemorial, the human collective has dabbled in separation consciousness, in this realm of relativity. We have purposely, as a collective humanity, forgotten who we truly are. This was deliberately done by us as a human collective, to have this Earth experience. However, the divine plan has shifted now, and we have exhausted and played out every possible scenario in separation consciousness we as a collective humanity were able to play out. We have each had many different character roles we have taken on each lifetime.

In other words, we have played this game all the ways it can be played, and it is time for a new experience. Therefore, by divine decree, there is something new ushering in now to take its place. A major shift is occurring within humanity and the earth. This shift some refer to as The Grand Awakening.

A New Earth has been created and now we, as a collective humanity, are beginning to awaken out of this dream state of amnesia we have purposely put ourselves in. It is a process and each person's awakening journey is different and divinely perfect for them. There is no one formula that fits all. However, in saying that, there are universal laws always at play, and have always been and will always be. We are all operating under these laws, whether we are conscious of it or not.

Mother Earth has made her shift and a New Earth has been birthed and exists now. She is graciously waiting for us to awaken and join her, as many already have. This process of awakening, the fulfillment of the divine plan, is occurring now on Earth and within humanity. When one begins to awaken, aligning themselves with the fulfillment of the divine plan, a healing journey begins for that being.

As you begin to raise your consciousness, knowing who you truly are, and holding a higher light frequency in your body and being, you begin to shed that which no longer serves you. You also begin to reclaim parts of self you may have resisted or pushed away in the past.

When you awaken, you become one with a higher consciousness and a knowing that all is Love, all is God, all is The Creative Source, and is who you are. You remember you have always been whole, therefore these parts you have pushed away, possibly for many lifetimes, must be integrated back into the wholeness you have always been. It is similar to going on a scavenger hunt, collecting and reclaiming, loving and accepting all of those parts of self you denied from your love in previous incarnations or even this incarnation.

Along with reclaiming parts of yourself you have withheld love from and embracing them once again, you also simultaneously begin to release that which no longer serves you. Some of these things to release may include limiting beliefs, old ways of being, old patterns, and anything blocking you in any way from embracing the fullness of your light, your true self, the pure unconditional love you have always been at your core. This is different for each person as we have all had varied life experiences in various incarnations.

It is a blessing, and it is comforting to know we are never alone in our journey. There are so many divine beings of infinite love and light assisting humanity and the planet itself at this pivotal time in Earth's history. However, nothing is more important and more valuable to you than the forging of the most intimate relationship you possibly can with your own "Mighty, Beloved I AM Presence."

You are God itself, one with all things, and the All is also one with you. Your "I AM Presence" is your own personal, individualized aspect of God. It has always been with you and will remain with you for all of eternity itself. It is your best friend. It is the only, and I will repeat, it is the *only* invincible solver of any perceived problem or situation you could ever have. We are each, in this Grand Awakening, remembering we are not here on this mission alone. It is not our job to figure anything out ourselves. In fact, it is the opposite. It is our job to remember to hand over absolutely everything we feel we have to grapple with, to our own "Mighty, Beloved I AM Presence."

We are so used to living in separation consciousness, somehow thinking we are separate from our Source.

You could never be separate from your Source. Your Source is the one who beats your heart, who breathes for you, who is your source for everything and all. This is your "I AM Presence." It loves you unconditionally beyond measure and it is waiting for you to turn to it and hand over any perceived problems or issues. As Archangel Raphael said to me once, "It is not a difficult thing to do, it takes diligence and a stick-to-itiveness."

It is a remembering to surrender and give your full authority and obedience to your own "I AM Presence." This allows your own "Mighty I AM Presence" to act through you and do all things for you with divine perfection on your behalf.

This takes effort and diligence, but it is not difficult. We have done things one way for so long and now we are switching gears, so it will take tenacity and discipline. It is as simple as remembering with your pure intention, to love and accept what is arising in your experience and then to hand it over, *surrender it*, to your "I AM Presence." As certain situations arise in your life, take a moment to breathe, be with it, send it love, and honor it as divine, merge with it because it is one with you, and then hand the whole situation immediately over to the only one who can solve the perceived problem you may be experiencing. Your "I AM Presence" always acts with, and is, divine perfection. Where your "I AM Presence" is, there is no time, as everything is the eternal now. Therefore, you can trust your calls are answered spontaneously and instantly.

The Divine is continuously bombarding the planet now with light for the highest good of all and for the divine plan fulfilled. Many human beings are awakening as we speak, and along with this, from The Divine, come many tools available to you to assist in your personal awakening process. As you remember to surrender to your own "Mighty I AM Presence" and intend to give it your full obedience and authority, you will find your journey is one of peace and divine ease and grace.

One of the most important things is to constantly turn inward to your own "Mighty I AM Presence" and ask it, with your intent, for everything and all you require. If there is anything you cannot figure out, if you need advice, if you need information, if you need help of any kind, your own "I AM Presence" is right there with you listening and waiting for your call.

I will be honest with you, it takes practice because we have all been trying to do things and figure things out on our own, looking to the external to find our answers. Therefore, it takes getting used to the truth that you have an invisible partner right there with you who is ready to fulfill your every desire and need as long as it serves your highest good and the highest good of all and is constructive and aligned with divine will. How amazing it is to know you are never alone and you have your own "I AM Presence" to fulfill your every need and desire if you acknowledge it and accept it as your own Mighty God Within, your Pure Christ, your Source for your being and life and All That Is?

The new ushers in now,
In its perfect time and way.
With blessings fulfilled,
It has birthed a new day.

Gone are the ways,
Of what has been before.
The door is now locked,
It is no more.

A glorious new dawn,
Rises for all.
A divine plan to be fulfilled,
You hear the call.

The releasing of the old,
To make space for the new.
A planting of seeds,
And wishes come true.

A grand wave is now here.
And it will not cease to be.
It is the Light,
Come to set you free!

So, turn inward beloved,
Doing the work now at hand,
And ride the wave,
And be not buried in the sand.

It is the grandest gift given,
That ever could be,
The awakening of your Mastery,
Your remembrance of me.

"I AM That I AM."

Recently, some amazing sacred texts have come into my awareness which The Great Masters of Light say are adorned in jewels in the Ascended Masters' Octave of Light. These texts have ushered in a whole new level of awareness for me. I had heard of them a long time ago in conversation, while I was visiting Mount Shasta, but had never actively followed through with purchasing them. However, this time was very different. It was clear to me they had arrived in perfect divine time and order for my further study and teachings in my remembrance of who it is I AM.

For me, they are an Ascended Masters guidebook. They are instructions from the Great Ascended Masters of Light, and other Great Divine Beings of Light on how to specifically *make the call,* as the masters refer to it. This *call* is an invoking of the powers from their great realms of light, and from the Great Central Sun, to bring forth into this physical octave support for the dissolving of density and discord on this planet and within humanity.

Since we each have divine free will, we must call forth this great light and power from the Masters' octave to consume and dissolve that which is of wrong creation here on Earth. This is the only way it can be done. The Light from the higher octaves must come forth by our very call to consume all wrong creations not serving the highest good of all. The Great Beings of Light and Pure Unconditional Love implore us, for our own sake, to make these calls.

This Light from the Ascended Masters' Octave, this Sacred Fire from the Great Central Sun, which is the life of Source itself, is indestructible, immortal, and pure. There is absolutely nothing of human creation that can survive or stay where it lives and abides. These sacred texts, *The "I AM" Discourses*, help you to remember this truth and teach you ways to enfold yourself in this invincible Sacred Fire Love, so you can move through this world untouched by all human appearances and human creations of lower frequencies, generated by the ego mind. It allows you to become a fountain of light, spouting forth wherever you abide, move, and go; the light awakens and frees all.

All are welcome to join those that are making these calls to assist humanity. This is the only way humans will gain their freedom by using the love and light called forth from the higher octaves of light. Also, it's important to call upon, with your pure intent, the light from the Ascended Masters' Octave into all outer world conditions to instantly dissolve and consume all that is of discord on this entire planet and to hold command with love so no further discord can create havoc for humanity and the Earth.

The fulfillment of the divine plan is underway now. It involves as many of us as possible to make these invocations, *making the call,* to bring forth the light and love that is The Sacred Fire of Love's indestructible, immortal, purity from The Great Central Sun. This Sacred Fire Love is the "Beloved, Mighty I AM Presence" and is the same love that also dwells within each person's heart center. You are a divine being of eternal love and light, and as such, you have the absolute authority to make these calls.

All is divine,
Of that you can be sure.
You are in one reality,
But there are, oh, so many more.

What appears to be so real,
Is the illusion you see,
And the characters we all play,
Are for the magnificent experience to be.

Divine magical fairies,
Unicorns and dragons are alive and well.
The illusion that we are in,
Can sometimes cast a spell.

A spell that can make us forget,
The love we truly are.
A spell that can cast you a drift,
Oh, so very far.

But never you be in worry,
And never you be in fear...
For by divine decree,
The time is now here.

A time to remember,
A place within your heart.
A place where you and I,
Have never been apart.

I love you.

TAKEAWAYS FOR YOUR TOOLBOX

The divine plan fulfilled is the awakening to the knowing that you are the Master of your own energy. It is a remembering of how to command energy. All of creation and existence is love energy, the "Mighty I AM Presence." As you regain your mastery of it, no longer are you controlled or plagued by the chatter of the lower mental mind, or any disturbance not based in love. To regain your mastery of energy is not difficult, it only takes diligence and determination. Mastery of energy and of all human creation takes your awareness and knowledge of the Laws of the Universe, which are always at play, and it takes your constant application of them.

You are not alone in this quest. There are teams of beings of infinite love and light, here now at your beck and call, to assist you and the planet with all things constructive for the fulfillment of the divine plan. However, you must initiate that call with your own authority and pure intention because we each have free will. The gifts you are blessed with by surrendering to your own "Mighty I AM Presence" and assisting The Great Beings of Light in the fulfillment of the divine plan are beyond measure.

Since there is only one of us here in truth, you are serving yourself when you serve another. You cannot help but be blessed with the same blessings you are calling forth for others. They are all you.

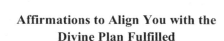

Affirmations to Align You with the
Divine Plan Fulfilled

I AM commanding, demanding, and intending, I AM the *Victory* of the divine plan fulfilled; so be it, and so it is.

I AM commanding, demanding, and intending, I AM the *Victory* of fully acknowledging and joyfully accepting my "Mighty God Within," my Pure Christ, now and for all eternity itself sustained; so be it, and so it is.

I AM commanding, demanding, and intending, I AM the *Victory* of giving all my authority and full obedience to my "Beloved, Mighty I AM Presence"; so be it and so it is.

I AM commanding, demanding, and intending there is but one, and I AM that one, now and for all eternity sustained; so be it, and so it is.

I AM commanding, demanding, and intending, I AM the *Victory* of surrendering all shadow thoughts from my thinking mind, and all discordant energies from my feeling world, to my "Beloved, Mighty I AM Presence" to be instantaneously dissolved and consumed in the light of my "I AM That I AM," the Cosmic Light Substance from the Great Central Sun; so be it, and so it is.

I AM commanding, demanding, and intending, I AM the *Victory* of asking my "Mighty I AM Presence" to ever charge me with its perfect, divine health, now and for all eternity itself sustained; so be it, and so it is.

I AM commanding, demanding, and intending, I AM the *Victorious light and the Victorious Christ*, wherever I abide, move, and go, now and for all eternity itself sustained; so be it, and so it is.

I AM commanding, demanding, and intending, I AM the *Victory* of ever being divinely guided by the light in my open, pure, grateful, appreciative heart; so be it, and so it is.

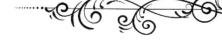

Saint Germain's Violet Flame, The Tube of Light, and The Law of Forgiveness

"This book must include Saint Germain and his energy of the Violet Flame," I heard, as a thought came swiftly into my awareness. I was almost certain I had placed in my book everything that needed to be included. Ahhh, but I was mistaken. I know how important Ascended Master Saint Germain is and his energy of the Violet Flame he so lovingly shares with each of us if we invoke it with our intention.

I cannot recall the first time I learned about the Violet Flame and how to put it to good use for myself. It feels to me I've always known about it, and I've always used it regularly. As a matter of fact, there is not one day that goes by that I do not invoke it. I do, however, remember one particular occasion early in my awakening journey when I invoked the Violet Flame, and it assisted me.

After I became certified in Integrative Energy Therapy, I attended several expos and conducted healings on people who had signed up for them. I also conducted healings at my home for some close friends. One day, a friend came over to my home and asked for healing.

This is the process whereby a facilitator works in cooperation with the nine healing angels to release the issues from a person's tissues. It is the clearing away of discordant energy in one's energy field with the assistance of the divine angelic realm.

My friend lay down on my massage table, and I proceeded to begin the healing process. I called in the nine angels of healing, and I also made sure to invoke protection for myself and for her. As I began the process, she started to tremble and shake quite a bit. I knew, in that moment, the nine healing angels were clearing something major out of her energy field. She had spoken to me prior to the healing, telling me she had been feeling down and didn't know why. During the healing process, discord or negative energy of any kind is drawn out of the person receiving the healing and it moves through the facilitator and then to the angels where it is then transmuted. It is never meant to get stuck within the one facilitating the healing.

I, too, was on my healing journey at the time, and I also had issues to heal within myself. I feel this is why this occurred next. As this energy cleared from my friend, it left her energy field and went into mine and stopped there. It was an entity of some sort. My whole body was buzzing with this unwelcome energy. It was very uncomfortable.

The thought of using the Violet Flame immediately came into my awareness. I lay down and invoked the Violet Consuming Flame, envisioning the purple flame passing up through my feet and continuing up throughout my whole body and out the top of my head. In an instant, I felt the flame, consuming and transmuting whatever this intrusive energy was.

I was so relieved and happy the Violet Flame worked spontan-eously, swiftly, and powerfully. I vowed from that day on to always use it. It can consume and transmute any discordant energy whatsoever not serving your highest good that is less than divine perfection, less than the perfection of your own "I AM Presence."

Saint Germain is and has been for eons the guardian of the Violet Flame. He has been upholding this Flame of Freedom for the planet for over 70,000 years. He is an awesome, dedicated Master in Service to all humanity.

Within the spiritual hierarchy, Saint Germain holds the position of the Cohan of the Seventh Ray. He is the guardian of the Violet Flame for Freedom and Transmutation for the planet, which is the action of the Seventh Ray. The Violet Flame is not one ray by itself. It is a combination of the blue for power and the pink for pure unconditional love. This unites the energies of the divine feminine and the divine masculine in a wondrous action of divine alchemy.

The main role of the Violet Flame is transmutation, a positive change.

By working and invoking the Violet Flame, you can transmute huge amounts of karma or misqualified energy and even dis-ease from this and past incarnations.

Once the energy has been transmuted by the Violet Flame, you do not have to deal with it again in your present life because those energies have been enfolded back into Source, into pure unconditional love with the use of the Violet Fire. As you begin to work with the Violet Flame, it dissolves all unbalanced, toxic, discordant, negative energies of all kinds in your auric field, as well as in your conscious, subconscious, and unconscious mind. It can heal many conditions in your life. The Violet Flame can be very advantageous for you to invoke every day, if not several times throughout the day or whenever you feel called to do so.

There are many ways in which you can use the Violet Flame constructively and effectively. You can use it through prayer and invocations, you can also visualize it in your meditation and set your intention to receive an infusion of the Violet Flame in all aspects of your being. Breathe it into every cell, atom, and electron of your body. Use it to purify your thinking mind and feeling world. Allow yourself to get creative and invoke it in a way that is personal for you, from your own heart.

Invocation to the Violet Flame

In the name of the I AM of my being, in the name of God, I now call forth the action of the Violet Flame of transmutation, compassion, and forgiveness in my auric field, for the cleansing and purifying of every thought and feeling in my solar plexus and in all my chakras. I ask the action of the Violet Fire to permeate every cell, atom, and electron of my four body systems, *the physical, emotional, mental, and spiritual beings and bodies*, at this moment and at all times each day of my life, twenty-four hours a day, seven days a week for the healing of all distortions in my energy fields from past and present misunderstandings. I ask the energies of the Violet Fire to start healing all distortions in my physical, emotional, mental, spiritual, energetic, and etheric beings and bodies. With much gratitude, I now ask for the action of the Violet Fire to manifest in my energy fields in full power. And so be it, and so it is.

I AM a Being of Violet Fire Visualization

As you say this decree, visualize the Violet Flame bathing and cleansing your aura. See the flames dissolving the debris in and around it.

I AM a being of Violet Fire; I AM the purity God desires.

You say this because you want to purify your aura of everything that is not of God. When you give this decree, visualize any negative energy that contacts these flames being instantly transmuted into the light of God.

Violet Flame Decree

I AM a being of Violet Fire!

I AM the purity God desires!

Below is a variation of this decree to insert the names of people you know or your hometown, nation, or the planet.

Earth is a planet of Violet Fire!

Earth is the purity God desires!

(Your city's name) is a city of Violet Fire!

(Your city's name) is the purity God desires!

Human beings' thoughts are almost never still. Individuals constantly develop ideas or thoughts within the forcefield of their own consciousness or they become subject to the thoughts of others, from thoughts floating in the atmosphere. Some of these thoughts are not harmful but some may not serve one's highest good. The safest thing for a student of the light is to understand the need to protect themselves from the random thoughts of others. The best way to do this is to simply invoke the "Tube of Light" from the heart of your own "Beloved Mighty I AM Presence."

No human can be free from his or her own human creations (those creations that are from the ego mind, less than love and above) unless each one will call upon his or her own God Presence, their "Mighty I AM Presence" to establish the Tube of Light, with their own intent, all about and around that one, wherever they abide, move and go! Then, with their pure intent, call and invoke the Violet Consuming Flame within that Tube of Light, to pass up through their feet and up through their whole physical body, through their mental and feeling world. Envision it like a great blowtorch that gives a great sense and feeling of accomplishment. Next, they allow the Violet Flame, now within the Tube of Light, where it is they now are, to instantaneously dissolve and consume every discordant thing, all discordant energy, all wrong creations and human creations (those of the ego mind) which have ever been drawn about them and accumulated through all their activities and embodiments.

Saint Germain has gifted us the exercise of the Tube of Light to energize our outer self. It has been told to us by Saint Germain during the Golden Ages, as we are all eternal beings of light, we used to live within this natural enfolding of oval light. When this Tube of Light is about you, no discord of Earth can pass through it. Over time, the Tube of Light we had all around each of us was destroyed. We are each being asked now to utilize this magnificent tool for our own highest good.

The Violet Consuming Flame and the Tube of Light are magnificent divine gifts we have been blessed with to set us free from all discord. I personally invoke the Tube of Light and the Violet Consuming Flame twice daily. However, I recommend tuning in and listening to your own "I AM Presence" as to how often you should invoke these magnificent gifts.

The Tube of Light

Beloved "I AM Presence" bright,
Round me, seal your Tube of Light.
From Ascended Master Flame,
Called forth now in God's own name.

Let it keep my temple free,
From all discord sent to me.
I AM calling forth Violet Fire,
To blaze and transmute all desire.

Keeping on in Freedom's name,
Till I AM one with the Violet Flame.

The Law of Forgiveness

The Violet Flame is a forgiving flame. It is not always easy, but without spiritual forgiveness, we cannot make spiritual progress. When we refuse to forgive someone for something, we tie ourselves not only to that person but to his/her anger as well.

Therefore, we are not truly free until we resolve the anger and balance the karma. Spiritually speaking, each time we do not forgive someone we are creating a barrier between ourselves and another part of God, who we are one with. There is a higher perspective that is not always easy to gain awareness of if one has experienced something leading them to be unforgiving of something or someone. However, no matter how bad a situation is perceived, or how you feel that a person's deeds are, it is for your highest good to always forgive the soul, thereby avoiding a karmic entanglement. Hatred binds and love always frees. We are all truly one; therefore, not forgiving another is not forgiving self.

It is also a very good practice, for your highest good, to forgive yourself for all those you may have wronged, and to forgive all others who may have wronged you, surrendering and releasing the entire situation into the hands of your "Mighty I AM Presence."

Please understand no matter what mistakes may have been, there is not a single thing unable to be remedied if you call upon the Law of Forgiveness. Pour your love first and foremost to your own "Mighty I AM Presence." Then call your own "Mighty I AM Presence" into action, and with your intention, ask it to instantly and spontaneously dissolve and consume every discordant thing, every discordant energy, every wrong creation, and human creation ever drawn about you and accumulated through all your activities and embodiments. As told by the Great Masters of Light, it is then you will have your freedom!

You don't have to live in the limitations and mistakes you have made in the past. We have each lived many lifetimes whether we are aware of that truth or not. Can you even imagine the accumulation of mistakes one could have possibly made in all those lifetimes combined? Now call to mind your own "Beloved, Mighty I AM Presence" who, through the application of these magnificent decrees, has provided a means by which in a few weeks or months, or even quicker, you can literally dissolve and consume every discordant thing accumulated about you through all those centuries.

Never has an opportunity arisen in this world, as the opportunity that stands before us all now to utilize these powerful decrees to free ourselves. The Great Masters have explained the Great Law, and the means to one's freedom, which has been presented to all of humankind through these decrees. It is now up to us whether we use them. If one chooses not to use them, they will carry on in distress and limitation. However, if one chooses to work within the laws of the universe, part of which is invoking these powerful decrees, they will be free from everything that distresses them in any manner whatsoever.

Forgiveness Decree

I AM Forgiveness acting here,
Casting out all doubt and fear,
Setting me forever free,
With wings of Cosmic Victory.

I AM calling in full power,
For Forgiveness every hour,
To all life in every place,
I flood forth forgiving grace.

Summary

Sweet words of thought,
Bless my page,
As I write them down,
Like a trusted sage.

To paint a picture in words,
The color so clear,
This is the message,
I've chosen to hear.

"Give freely," it says,
"From a heart, pure and true.
For the blessing in truth,
I give only to you."

Do you know this?
Have you come to understand?
As you give to another,
I then place it all in your hand.

All you will allow,
And then even more.
Do you fully understand this?
Are you really sure?

There is but One.

You are the "Beloved, Mighty I AM Presence" and so is everything and everyone else on Earth and in all of creation and existence. You are pure unconditional love, and you are the light. You have always been love; you are love now, and you will always be love.

There is absolutely nothing but pure unconditional love, which is divine perfection, in all of creation and in all of existence, now and forevermore. You are an eternal being of light. You are magnify-icent, limitless, and boundless, and you are always worthy and deserving of all you desire.

We are all Master Creators of our own realities, and we are in the process of waking up out of separation consciousness, *the illusion*, into oneness consciousness, *the truth of All That Is*. We are waking up to embrace and to embody our whole, true selves, our own divinity. It is the process of shifting out of forgetfulness of who it is you truly are and into the remembrance of All That Is and has always dwelled within you.

The entire universe dwells within each of us. Your perceived reality reflects your inner beliefs about self, which are being mirrored back to you as a gift. As you awaken and remember your divinity, you begin the process known as *ascension*.

During this process of ascension, old beliefs, old patterns, old ways of being, and all not serving the embodiment of your true self falls away. You cease seeking answers outside of self, from the external world, and you begin to look inward turning first and foremost to your own "I AM Presence" for everything and for all. This enables the full embodiment of your "I AM Presence," your purest divine love essence. This is the part of you that knows only love and is only love.

Therefore, some beings may be what we call sound asleep, while others may be beginning to awaken, and still, there are others who have awakened thousands of years ago. It does not matter when you awaken. You will always do so when the time is divinely perfect for you. All is always in perfect divine time and order.

Everything and all you experience in your own reality is brought into your awareness by you. You may not be conscious of that knowing; however, it is true. You bring various experiences to assist yourself in growing in love and wisdom, to once again become who it is you already are—pure divine love.

These experiences, whether individual or at the collective level of humanity, will continue to come forward for you, as well as for the collective, until self and the collective awakens and embraces who it is we all are in truth. This involves a radical love and acceptance for all arising in your reality, whether in your personal life or on the world stage, to be seen and heard and loved.

We are all evolving, and we are all expanding to higher light in each moment. We are always each seeking the full embodiment with the highest aspect of who it is we are. Absolutely everything and all is about that.

A key to living in oneness, which in turn can translate to a life of pure bliss, perfect health, abundance, and joy and all your desires made manifest, is to only be and do what feels good to you.

This, at first to some, may appear to be a selfish act, but it is exactly the opposite on the deepest level. Since there is only one of us here in truth, when you always follow your own joy, it automatically serves the highest good for all involved. This is true because there is absolutely no separation.

We are all extensions of Source Energy, one whole body of love. We play out these seemingly separate, specific character roles we have each chosen for ourselves before incarnating.

In the beginning of one's awakening journey, sometimes clearly seeing we are all truly one can be a difficult truth to embrace. We are so varied and diversified in the roles we have assigned ourselves on Earth. The character or role you play this lifetime is what you specifically chose for yourself.

The Creative Source of All That Is, your own "I AM Presence," is experiencing itself in all its infiniteness. As extensions of Source Energy, we are experiencing ourselves through the specific roles each of us have chosen for ourselves.

This is a co-creation. It is a partnership, and you are not here to do anything alone. You could not be or do anything alone even if you tried because you are The Creative Source itself. However, people can forget (and most *have* forgotten), they are The Creative Source of All That Is here to experience itself in all its infiniteness.

The experience of forgetfulness is also divinely orchestrated by us as a human collective. We chose, as the one Source we are, to forget for the sake of the experience. We did this so we could find our own way back to the love we each are, all whilst allowing ourselves to have the experience of the senses and all the adventures that come along with it on this glorious planet of Earth.

We have experienced separation consciousness, forgetting the love we truly are, for a long while now. It is time to wake up now out of this particular adventure, out of this dream, out of this illusion that we are somehow separate from each other and separate from All That Is, our "I AM Presence."

There are infinite means by which one can come to the profound realization of who one truly is. It is important to honor your own journey as a sacred one, and it is also important to honor the journeys, and the free will of all others as well. We are all meant to be so different in the characters we play and yet we are also one and the same.

Love is the ultimate healer, and love is who you are. The author Matt Kahn titled his book *Whatever Arises, Love That*. This is the best advice one could carry out for oneself. All things are truly possible through acceptance of self and all else through divine love.

You are one with The Divine and therefore all things are always possible through and with you.

Allow yourself to take that leap of faith Archangel Michael asked me to take. It becomes such a joy and so much fun to discover the beauty, the mystery, and all the magic of who you truly are.

The children, the newest ones on the planet, experience their memory of All That Is as still being fresh and present within them. They see all through innocent perception with their childlike wonder and excitement. This is what is being asked of each of us now. It is a return to the remembrance of fun, play, wonder, and miracles.

It is important to mention none of us are victims of anything as the powerful Master Creators we are. Sometimes this can be a hard pill to swallow upon awakening to the truth of ourselves. When we wake up into oneness consciousness, we take full responsibility for everything that occurs in our lives. This is because we have summoned it all to ourselves for our own growth in love and wisdom, in the becoming of that which we already are: pure, divine love and light.

We also accept All That Is. This means whatever is showing up in our lives we take full responsibility, in the knowing that we, in fact, have brought it forth to wake us up to the greater truth of ourselves.

Everything you see around you and all that is your experience has already been manifested, it is old news. Therefore, allow yourself to be a dreamer of the reality you wish to create. We are meant to be conscious, deliberate creators of our own realities. We were never meant to focus our attention on *the old* and create more of the same. As we allow ourselves to embrace each moment as a new opportunity to bring forth our dreams, they are then able to manifest as we have made space for them to do so.

It is so important to allow your imagination to wander and to dream often. We can choose to dream and imagine a new reality for ourselves and a new reality for the collective humanity and for Mother Earth, our home. A reality that serves the highest good of all because there is no such thing as scarcity in oneness consciousness. For example, if everyone desires a blue car and aligns with their own "I AM Presence," they'd all be able to manifest it for themselves simultaneously.

If we choose, we can dream up, imagine, and manifest a New Earth where everything and all serves the highest good for ourselves, for all humanity and for Mother Earth. This is how we create the New Earth. When we focus on what has already been manifested, as we create our realities through our own thoughts, words, actions, and beliefs about things, we end up creating the same old circumstances and experiences.

That is how history can keep repeating itself. We never intended that for ourselves. We can instead envision and create a world where all are loved, living in abundance, and where the truth that we are one is known, embraced, and lived by all.

As we are each now planting seeds for the New Earth, it's important to allow yourself to dream. You are a boundless, limitless, vast, infinite, eternal, multidimensional being of infinite love and light. You are loved unconditionally beyond measure by The Divine now and forevermore, and all is truly well.

As Abraham always says through Ester Hicks, "We never can ever get it wrong, and we can never get it done."

We are eternal. When you know this as your truth, you can then relax, play, and allow yourself to be the joy you always have been at your core, your essence, all the time.

May you be infinitely blessed in the oneness of all things, and may you always know in your heart you are magnificent and divinely loved unconditionally beyond measure because of who you truly are.

Blessed be you,
In the energy of light.
Bathed in divine love,
You are held this night.

Just as a babe is soothed,
By its mother's tender embrace,
Swaddled and cared for,
By divine's holy grace.

Be you at peace,
And know this to be true,
There is no love greater,
Than the love I have for you.

Deep, deep down,
Where the wild things grow,
A magic field lies,
You well know.

It is a field of possibilities,
A playground of joy, of pure delight.
It is rich in merriment,
Where dreams take flight.

You have been there before,
Alas, you may forget,
Don't worry dear one,
I have cast my net.

I have cleared the path for you,
Of all stones and rubble,
You dear one,
Will have no trouble.

I wait for you,
In my field of treasure,
With a love for you,
You will never measure.

Acknowledgments

I would like to express my deepest heartfelt gratitude and appreciation to those who are very special to me. These *special ones* have helped me tremendously throughout my journey. Some of them are aware of the positive impact they have had in my life and others are not. However, I will forever be grateful to them all.

I express my love and gratitude to my friends and family, Holdyn (my son), William Burke (my father), Margaret Burke (my mother), Jeannie Welch, Sydney Welch, Kelly Kolodney, Simona Manenti, Honey Bellosi, Randen Seichick, Whalt Garcia, and Sharon Bowman.

I would also like thank you, Matt Kahn, for your mentorship.

I AM also pouring all my love and appreciation to my divine family of Light, my own "Beloved, Mighty, I AM Presence," Archangel Raphael, Archangel Michael, Ascended Master Yeshua, Lord Melchizedek, Ascended Master Merlin, Ascended Master Hilarion, Ascended Master Saint Germain, Ascended Master Mother Mary, Ascended Master Kuan Yin, and many, many more.

I express my deep gratitude to Michelle Vandepas, Karen Parker, and the entire team at GracePoint Publishing, and I would like to especially thank Lexi Mohney for all her help, care, and assistance in helping this book come to life. I AM grateful.

About the Author

Kim Barder is a mother, intuitive healer, poet, and author. She is currently serving the light, aligned with her "I AM Presence," alongside her Starseed Sisters and Brothers of Light, members of the Angelic Realm, and The Ascended Masters of Light and other Divine Cosmic Beings of Light who are all aligned with pure unconditional love and the "I AM That I AM Presence," bringing forth the raising of consciousness for herself, the human collective, and Mother Earth, all for the highest good of all.

Kim creates poetry and writings which facilitate healing on a soul level, always through the divine guidance of her "I AM Presence." Kim's pursuits have their essence in unity, authentic power, connection, resonance with love, and the "I AM That I AM" in the unified field of One.

She also loves walks on the beach, a good cup of tea, and a great book to read.

Resources

Anna, Grandmother of Jesus by Claire Heartsong

Anna, The Voice of the Magdalenes by Claire Heartsong in creation with Catherine Ann Clemett

The Ascension Flame of Purification and Immortality by Aurelia Louise Jones

The Book of Knowledge: The Keys of Enoch by J.J. Hurtak

Conversations with God by Neal Donald Walsch

The 'I AM' Discourses by Guy Ballard

I Remember Union by Flo Aeveia Magdalena

Love Without End by Glenda Greene

Prayers to the Seven Sacred Flames by Aurelia Louise Jones

The Seven Sacred Flames by Aurelia Louise Jones

Whatever Arises, Love That by Matt Kahn

Website References

www.simonamanenti.com

www.theangelraphael.com

www.sacredscribesangelnumbers.blogspot.com

www.mattkahn.org

www.soulutionsfordailyliving.com

www.nealedonaldwalsch.com

www.theiamdiscourses.com

For more great books from Peak Press
Visit Books.GracePointPublishing.com

If you enjoyed reading *Now, I AM* and purchased it through an online retailer, please return to the site and write a review to help others find the book.

Printed in Great Britain
by Amazon

31736792R00152